One Minute with GOD for Women

HOPE LYDA

HARVEST HOUSE PUBLISHERS

EUGENE, OREGON

Cover by Garborg Design Works, Savage, Minnesota

ONE MINUTE WITH GOD FOR WOMEN GIFT EDITION
Copyright © 2008 by Hope Lyda
Published 2011 by Harvest House Publishers
Eugene, Oregon 97402
www.harvesthousepublishers.com

ISBN 978-0-7369-3038-3

Printed in China

14 15 16 17 18 / RDS-NI / 10 9 8 7 6

Contents

Just a Minute...

One minute? That's what you allot an egg to be cooked for breakfast, a commercial to entice you, a meter to keep you ticket free for a quick stop. So one minute with God seems a bit...meager. Ah, but a minute can turn into so much more.

You're busy. You probably send up prayers throughout the day asking for a second pair of hands, patience in the bank line, and energy for a task. But when you turn your focus to God for a minute, your heart opens up to his hope for your future and his vision for your life.

May these brief devotions and prayers become the breathing space you long for during your busiest days. God's presence is a sanctuary you'll want to return to more and more as one minute transforms into a lifetime of connection with your Creator.

Transformation

Words of Transformation

The way to become wise is to honor the LORD;
he gives sound judgment to all
who obey his commands.

PSALM 111:10 TEV

Jesus called a child to come and stand in front
of them, and said, "I assure you that unless
you change and become like children, you
will never enter the Kingdom of heaven."

MATTHEW 18:2-3 TEV

Some, however, did receive him and believed
in him; so he gave them the right to become
God's children. They did not become
God's children by natural means, that is,
by being born as the children of a human
father; God himself was their Father.

JOHN 1:12-13 TEV

What is mortal must be changed into
what is immortal; what will die must
be changed into what cannot die.

1 CORINTHIANS 15:53 TEV

Keep your roots deep in him, build your lives on him, and become stronger in your faith, as you were taught. And be filled with thanksgiving.

COLOSSIANS 2:7 TEV

All things are done according to God's plan and decision; and God chose us to be his own people in union with Christ because of his own purpose, based on what he had decided from the very beginning. Let us, then, who were the first to hope in Christ, praise God's glory!

EPHESIANS 1:11-12 TEV

Perseverance must finish its work so that you may be mature and complete, not lacking anything.

JAMES 1:4

New Attitude

My friend is trying new things. New healthy habits. New ways of approaching her fears. New attitudes. These changes don't feel awkward to her; they feel familiar, comfortable, a perfect fit. Funny how it takes change, small and big, internal and external, for you to become more like yourself—to fit the heart and purpose God gave you from the very beginning.

If you set out to "find yourself," you're headed for a long road with many twists and intersections. And an elusive destination. But when you embark on a journey to find who you are in God, the destination is unwavering. You'll feel more like your true self with each step you take.

I want to find the way to the fulfilling life you have planned for me, God. With each change or decision that I turn over to your guidance, I know I will come closer to the "me" you created.

Change of Path

Our brains create routes to memories, emotions, ideas, and responses. These serve us well, unless those embedded routes lead us to crumbled roads of routine anger, depression, and self-deception. When we embrace faith, God's grace renews our minds and hearts; we're no longer stuck in or imprisoned by old behaviors and thoughts.

Have you experienced this infusion of hope and transformation? It might take time for your broken thinking and broken living to be replaced by God's truth and peace. But your prayers for new patterns are heard. And new ways are being shaped in you. Trust the changes that usher you toward a whole faith.

God, create new ways for me to approach life, hope, and my future. When my past hurts lead to broken thinking, renew my thoughts. Fill my mind with the hope of faith and the peace of a transformed heart.

Finding Your Voice

Do you know what you sound like? Beyond the voice you use to ask for help around the house or to request a memo at work. What do you say to yourself when silence surrounds you and thoughts start swirling? These are often the moments when your true voice emerges. It reminds you of your faith, your value, your gifts, and your dreams. And God knows that voice—he hears it when you pray, when you struggle, when you silently call out for help, when you lift up a secret hope.

A woman's life is transformed when she rediscovers the voice God gives her. Allow time to hear it and to treasure it.

You know the sound my heart makes when it calls out to you. You've heard my tears fall and seen my hopes rise. Lead me to know my voice and to use it to proclaim your goodness.

The Redemption of Flaws

What about your behavior gets old—even to you? I'll start with a few from my list of sometimes-annoying attributes: shyness, sarcasm, indecisiveness, messiness…When left unpolished and jagged, these behaviors work against my purpose. But when given over to God's grace, they're like the bit of sand wedged in an oyster's home…transformed over time and effort into a pearl. My indecisiveness will never be lovely, but the transformed version will be.

What does your spouse or friend or coworker do that rubs you the wrong way? Give those, too, to God; let irritation lead to transformation in you and in your relationships.

There's so much I do that can drive me nuts.
I'm sorry for the times when my example is such
a shallow representation of your holiness. May
I turn over to you each of my less-than-lovely
characteristics so that I can become more like you.

Ongoing Education

Did you miss class this week? God's class is always going on. And there were quite a few lessons to be learned in the past few days. How much of your faith education do you miss because you aren't aware, taking notes, or showing up for your life?

In a very miraculous way, God is always bringing teachers to our paths. We'll learn new ways to hope and help, and skills to grow in faith and compassion. We never finish discovering more about how life and faith intersect, how God loves, and how we're to love others. In fact, when we naively say "I've arrived!" a big life lesson is about to hit!

Let me watch for the teachers you bring into my life. I'm so thankful for those who reach out to me when I need connection, those who express your wisdom when I struggle, and those who stand firm when I'm floundering. Help me to glean truth from these examples.

Between Here and There

Travels to a foreign land or a nearby town or a rarely visited forest offer opportunities to depend on God in new ways. I've been places where I didn't know the language and had to rely on God's leading to make the journey safely. He'd reroute me with a tug of intuition when I'd wander. He'd present the person or form of transportation I needed.

Each time I travel, God gives me the vision to see his interaction with me on a very personal level. I never feel closer to him than when I'm totally dependent. Even if you don't have plane tickets tucked away for an upcoming adventure, rely on God for your daily needs, direction, shelter, connections with people, etc. The gift of travel graces is a part of your everyday life.

Help me to depend on you for everything, God. When I feel like I know what to expect, I start to rely on my strength rather than your power. I truly am a visitor journeying through this life. I need to act like it!

The Unfolding of a Life

Life's always changing around us. Friends take new jobs, move across the country, start families, get divorced, watch kids leave, discover their passions, come to faith, question God, and on and on. Do you feel such shifts happening in your own life? Or do you resist change as much as possible because you don't want to disturb your sense of security?

When each day looks the same, when your calendar for this year matches that of last year, when your wish list, group of friends, or menu of struggles and grudges is exactly the same, it's time for change. I know change is hard. But by fearfully avoiding potentially bad stuff, you've avoided the good stuff. Allow your life to unfold.

I'm ready to view change as a good thing. I've fought transitions in the past because they made me feel alone and out of control. I tried to control the outcome rather than turn it over to you. This change I'm facing...I'll see it as an opportunity.

Take Your Own Advice

"Just be yourself!" We speak this affirmation with fervent enthusiasm to others who are feeling left out because of their uniqueness or perceived weaknesses. We champion the underdog with the phrase because something about it resounds with truth in our hearts. We believe it. We do. But do we believe it in a big way for our own lives?

We'll go to great lengths to be like others, to become special editions of ourselves (only the ideal parts), or to present airbrushed versions (only the fake, ideal parts). When will we love who we are? Yes, we can improve. Yes, we'll still experience transformation. But we are to be ourselves—*this* is what makes faith and life work. "Just be yourself" is a call to know yourself as God does.

When will I accept the me you know and love? I've tried to pursue paths that were not mine to pursue. I've longed for dreams that weren't mine to entertain. And I've pushed myself to be something I'm not. It feels good to be back here as myself. As your child.

Let It Rise

What potential is forming in your heart and spirit that needs nurturing? You think of it when you're standing in line, wiping the counter, folding laundry, typing an email. It breaks into your thoughts with a flash and disappears into the mundane. But this elusive idea longs to be given weight and dimension, and the time it takes to gain such importance.

Let what is becoming rise up in you. Give it attention, a quiet place to rest, and encouragement when it is ready to take shape. Don't brush aside these pieces of yourself. God leads you to truths that are waiting to rise up and become parts of your life.

I'm rarely silent enough to hear your still small voice. But when I focus, close my mouth, and open my heart, I sense your leading. I'm amazed when I get a glimpse of the dream you're shaping in me, God.

Which Way?

I ask God for a clearer sign to identify where I'm at and where I might be headed. If I'm on the road less traveled, I question why more people haven't thought to go this route if it is of such value. When I'm rushing alongside the masses on the highway of success, ambition, or status quo, then I wonder why more people don't think to leave this chaos.

Which road are you on? Do you look around at your home, your family, and your job and wonder if you are on God's intended path? Rest in today. Rest in the choices you've made that have directed you here. Do not give God your "what ifs" as an offering; instead, give him your commitment to go forward with faith and peace.

Which way, God? Others around me are choosing paths, some with certainty and some with timidity. I want to experience the peace of moving forward. I know that when I trust you and rest in your faithfulness, I can walk with sure steps.

Renewal

Words of Renewal

He put a new song in my mouth,
a hymn of praise to our God.
Many will see and fear
and put their trust in the LORD.

PSALM 40:3

Create in me a pure heart, O God,
and renew a steadfast spirit within me.

PSALM 51:10

My soul finds rest in God alone;
my salvation comes from him.
He alone is my rock and my salvation;
he is my fortress, I will never be shaken.

PSALM 62:1-2

A generous man will prosper;
he who refreshes others will himself be refreshed.

PROVERBS 11:25

Even youths grow tired and weary,
and young men stumble and fall;
but those who hope in the Lord
will renew their strength.

Isaiah 40:30-31

Forget the former things;
do not dwell on the past.
See, I am doing a new thing!
Now it springs up; do you not perceive it?
I am making a way in the desert
and streams in the wasteland.

Isaiah 43:18-19

You were wearied by all your ways,
but you would not say, "It is hopeless."
You found renewal of your strength,
and so you did not faint.

Isaiah 57:10

I will give you a new heart and put a new
spirit in you; I will remove from you your
heart of stone and give you a heart of flesh.

Ezekiel 36:26

Real Freedom

Are you eager to have an exuberant, joyful faith? Do you want a faith that soars high above mediocrity? First, you might have to cut some ties that keep your growth and belief confined to worldly standards. There is someone you know (quite well, actually) who might be restricting you with limited power, understanding, and wisdom.

Okay, it's you! If you're relying on yourself to gain the freedom and joy of the Lord, you've probably gone as far as you can go. Get out from under your own control! And experience the real freedom of faith.

My own power is so limited. So is my wisdom and understanding. Why do I still think I should be in charge of my life? God, help me to release my grip on my days, my purpose, my future so that the real freedom of living in your strength becomes mine.

On a Limb

When you're used to clinging to things of the world to ground you, secure you to meaning, the life of belief can be scary! It can also be exhilarating. Even if you clung to the tree for a long time before stepping out on the limb of belief, you're an adventuress! You're learning to rely on God's strength and security with every step. And he faithfully takes you forward and shows you the vista of purpose from up on high.

Close your eyes, feel the breeze on your face, and reach out for God's leading. Experience the delight of this new kind of living.

There's much left for me to see, discover, learn, and celebrate! Each time I seek your will and strive to live abundantly, I am an adventuress. It's amazing to consider the heights to which you will take me and to know that the horizon ahead is one you created for me.

Bright Eyed

It's fun to watch the faces of people holding a baby. They stretch their smiles, purse their lips, and lift their eyebrows. They mirror what they're watching in the face of the infant. In that moment when bright eyes meet wide eyes, there's an uplifting of heart and soul.

If our journeys are reflecting the countenance of God, there'll be many moments of bright eyes and hopeful smiles. This day, this moment, is a part of God's amazing, miraculous creation. Mirror his delight in the gift of living!

God, do I reflect you in my life? Is there an expression I make or a gesture I extend that reflects your image? I want to show you to others, and I want to show you the joy of my faith.

Spiritual Makeover

Is your spiritual life sagging? Is a once-active faith now a matter of "doing the right thing"? As women, we give a lot to others. Even when this is done with willing, servants' hearts, it can cause us to ignore our living faith. If your belief system is more system than belief, it's time for a spiritual makeover.

Determine what's missing from your life with God. Maybe it's been years since you totally depended on him. Maybe you haven't prayed from a place of absolute need and hope. Walk into the presence of God. Ask for renewal of spirit, mind, body, and soul. Rejuvenate your faith.

God, more than I need to be right,
or perceived as perfect…I need you. I know that
the life of faith isn't about perfection. I want
to free myself from the expectations of others so
that I can live fully under the covering of your
hope and grace. Show me what's missing.

Refinish

If you've ever taken on the project of turning a drab piece of forgotten furniture into a showcase item for your home, you know how much work is involved in making something new again...or better than new. First you must strip away the build-up of finish and stains—long forgotten versions of what is aesthetic. Then you see that hint of newness and natural beauty; the result is a treasure.

Do other people's versions of beauty, worthiness, and value still cover your life? Do stains of sin and loss and pain dull your heart? With God's grace, you can remove those layers. It might take work, tears, and times of questioning, but the life that emerges will be the one God wants to see shine. It will be a treasure.

God, please strip away my layers of sin, mistakes, arrogance, stubbornness, and rebellion. They've obscured my purpose and beauty. When I try to do the right thing, it's often with selfish motives. I want the treasure of my faith and heart to be revealed.

Open to Be Filled

Why is it that when I have work to do that requires an attentive mind, all I want to do is paint a room or rearrange my bookshelf? Organizing my hall closet suddenly seems like the perfect afternoon activity. This frustrates me until I realize that I'm hungering for what I need. These activities feed me, fuel me, and allow me to settle once again into more focused work.

So it goes with the faith life. If you spend all your time analyzing how God works, contemplating the origin of the universe, and scrutinizing your commitment to faith, God is probably nudging you to take a breath, plant a flower, write a note, organize a kitchen cupboard, and allow yourself to be emptied so that you can then be filled with him.

Okay, it's hard for me to let go of some things. I'll think a question or concern to death and then wonder why I don't feel peace. Help me to see the world of beauty around me. May I be inspired to savor life and feel a renewal of my spirit.

Step Aside

The day can become all about what you say, what you do, where you put your car keys, the time you wasted looking for your car keys. But when you pause and consider life beyond you, you'll discover what God wants you to notice.

There are times when God asks you to live beyond your needs and the thoughts rolling about in your mind so that you can listen to others, meet their needs, hear their opinions, and learn about their journeys. Step aside for the day; be God's ears, eyes, and hands.

If I'd just look up from my to-do list and stop checking for voice mails, I'd notice the things you have for me to do. They aren't always a part of my human agenda. Who should I meet? What long-forgotten dream should I resurrect? Show me.

Useful

I decided to start composting this year. People who do it right end up with wonderful nourishment for their flowers, shrubs, and vegetables. I love it because my broken broccoli stems, wilted lettuce, and eggshells no longer stink up my kitchen's 13-gallon wastebasket. Instead, this leftovers cocktail will become useful material.

God, the Master Gardener, does a lot of composting in our lives. When we give him our debris—our wilted spirits, the shells of our egos, the broken pieces of our lives—he tends to them. He turns our losses and our sins into the useful material of faith.

My past mistakes are useless. They pile up and start to decay. Yet I walk around carrying them like it makes sense. I'm crazy. You're not only willing, but longing to take this debris from me and exchange it for beauty, direction, and peace. Please make my brokenness and wasted moments useful.

Starting Over

Some friends are dealing with divorce and its aftermath. Others are at the crossroads of choosing a new job or even a new profession. Moms face empty homes as grown children reach for their futures. Life is filled with transitions—some we hope for, some we avoid as long as possible. Give yourself over to the chance to start over!

There's so much to discover about yourself and God when you face transitions with your heart open to what the next opportunity has to offer. Sadly, many of us wait until *major* transitions take place before we trust in God's leading. Each choice, each dream, each hope, and each heartache can be given over to God's capable hands.

*Show me how to handle this transition with grace.
I'm a bit scared, and I certainly have a lot of doubt.
But you're ready to lead me. You take my shaky hand
and guide me through what seems like an ending
but becomes a beginning. A beautiful beginning.*

Breaktime

It's good to get away from the pressures of life. How often do you take a nap? a vacation? a bubble bath? It's breaktime—starting now. What will you do with it? What do you long for? What has God been placing on your heart—you know, the dream you ignore time after time?

When's the last time you gave yourself a break? Do you count up your indiscretions at the end of the day? Do you beat yourself up every time you slip and fall? There's a lot of living to be done on the other side of self-loathing. Give yourself a break, and discover the peace God offers.

As a kid, I'd wake from a nap with an eagerness for whatever came next. If I'd had a bad morning, I could easily start over after a good rest. As an adult, I need a break from my angst, my worries, and my self-reprimands so that I can eagerly receive your grace and your fresh plans for my life.

Patience and Peace

Words of Patience and Peace

I know, my God, that you test the heart
and are pleased with integrity.

1 Chronicles 29:17

Submit to God and be at peace with him;
in this way prosperity will come to you.
Accept instruction from his mouth
and lay up his words in your heart.

Job 22:21-22

The Lord gives strength to his people;
the Lord blesses his people with peace.

Psalm 29:11

Seek peace and pursue it.

Psalm 34:14

Consider the blameless, observe the upright;
there is a future for the man of peace.

Psalm 37:37

I wait for you, O LORD;
you will answer, O Lord my God.

PSALM 38:15

You will keep in perfect peace
him whose mind is steadfast,
because he trusts in you.

ISAIAH 26:3

[Jesus] got up, rebuked the wind and said
to the waves, "Quiet! Be still!" Then the
wind died down and it was completely
calm. He said to his disciples, "Why are you
so afraid? Do you still have no faith?"

MARK 4:39-40

We do not want you to become lazy, but to
be like those who believe and are patient,
and so receive what God has promised.

HEBREWS 6:12 TEV

Silence Is Golden

Light a candle. Draw the blinds. Turn off the television. Take a seat. Introduce yourself to silence. It can be uncomfortable at first. Even later on. But without it, your heart has no space to find God. The noises that create a constant soundtrack to your life need to be quieted once in awhile.

In the silence, your long-neglected worries, praises, hopes, and truths will rise up and be offered to the Lord. Don't drown out these heartfelt prayers.

Resting in your peace eases my soul. The endless questions and doubts stop midflight. My shoulders relax; they no longer have to bear all the burdens of my world. My heart calms; it no longer has to keep up with my unrealistic pace.

The Big Break

I know it'll happen any day now—the big break that will take my life to the next level of happiness, hope, and potential. Do you feel that too? Are you waiting for your big break? A sudden flood of cash, a career boost, a knight in shining armor, a launch to fame, the perfect alignment of time and money so that you can finally accomplish your dream?

Sometimes waiting is the practice of godly patience. Sometimes it is purely an act of futility—a deferment of living. Don't you know...while we're waiting for our respective big breaks, God is waiting for a break in our holding pattern? He's hoping we'll recognize the happiness, hope, and potential in the day we're living, the relationship we are in, and the dream we're walking toward.

When I'm waiting futilely for worldly success or recognition or an open door that has long been shut, help me to move on. Give me words of wisdom through others and through my time in prayer. I want to recognize my big break... my chance to live the big life of faith.

Waiting for What's There

Have you ever waited for a friend to call or make a move to show her loyalty? When you're feeling lonely, thoughts can shift to how others aren't available or attentive enough. You'll look for faults in others to find the reason for your own sadness. When night comes and you've been waiting all day for assurance, God's grace is here to cover you, his love is here to fill that void.

While you're looking for someone to blame or someone to save you from loneliness, God is with you. He is waiting for you to call on him.

I used to try and ignore the loneliness I'd feel from time to time. Or I'd pretend it related to how someone else was treating me or acting toward me. The truth is, my loneliness is often an ache for intimacy with you. Your love is meant to fill me.

Clarity

Anger and frustration rise up in me and take me by surprise. I'm short with strangers and curt with loved ones. I feel the need to get clarity. I've lost perspective. I need distance to witness what my behavior is and to keep it in check.

Does your attitude or lack of reason ever shock you? Let God be your outside perspective. He provides wake-up calls so that we get a glimpse of what he sees happening. His peace can calm our anger. His compassion can make us tender again. His grace allows us to speak with love. His perspective gives us the clarity we need to turn to him for help.

I don't always hear myself or see my actions clearly until I do something that is blatantly unkind. God, when I'm feeling edgy or irritated, help me bring my troubles to you. Help me search my heart for the source of the hurt, the indifference, or the anger.

A New Emphasis

It's difficult to notice the blessings in your life when all you see are the demands, expectations, responsibilities, and daily grind. Was there an actual point of exchange when you traded living for talking about, shopping for, plotting out, and managing a life?

Are you in this spot? There's a surprisingly simple remedy: Change the emphasis. Allow each day to be about living, not the strings attached that make it go. Give those to God. View your planner as a friend rather than a ruler. It's difficult to notice the demands, expectations, and responsibilities when all you see are the blessings.

No more just managing my life. I want to live it! My life's path is often all about what society demands of me. I want to hunger only for your requests of my time, heart, energy, talents, and soul. May I seek out your calling, and may I honor the blessings you provide.

Peace March

What do you stand for? Do your words express bitterness or forgiveness? Do you present the case for mercy or judgment? Do you extend hostility or hospitality? Do you side with the powerful or champion the weak? Do you remain silent, or do you speak out against injustice? Do you correct, or do you encourage? Do you hoard, or do you give? Do you expect, or do you offer? Do you pick apart others, or do you piece them together?

Are you willing to be a reflection of Christ? Move forward in faith. Start walking toward a life that stands for something.

My heart needs to be softened, Lord. I become jaded too easily. I want my daily actions and words to reflect a spirit of peace, compassion, and tenderness. I long to stand for your goodness by showing unconditional love and endless mercy.

My Blankie!

Hand it over. I know you have one—an adult version of a blankie. No? Take a look at what you reach for every time you need a sense of security. When things spin out of control, what comforts you? There are many security blankets that clutter our existence, even as rational adults—food, work, sex, television, computer games, emails, material possessions, shopping for those possessions, lashing out at others, and so on.

Our temporal options feel good initially, but as is the nature of things of the world…they become tattered, ineffective substitutions for God's peace. When you need assurance, comfort, and an anchor to purpose, reach for the blanket of God's grace and security.

I don't wanna let go! This security blanket has seen me through trials in my work and my relationships. It was with me when I had an identity crisis. But I know it's time to relinquish my hold…it will never be a substitute for my assurance in and of you.

Small Talk

I talk to God about the hidden part of my soul, the darkest corner of my fear, and the brightest spark of my hope. But now and then I'll start with small talk, like we've just met. I'll stammer a bit, discuss the weather, or what I'm going to do tomorrow. Then God gives me his peace. He reassures me that anything I say is important to him.

And just like that, I move from shallow conversation to the deep waters of soulful prayer. I can barely contain myself, because I want him to know all of me, and I want to know all of him. Are you caught in a cycle of small talk? God is with you, and he's nodding, smiling, and waiting—not to be entertained by you—but to be trusted and known.

God, I'm here with the good and the bad. I want to get personal and real and intimate with you. You picked the colors of my soul. You know me when I am scared to know myself. Are you ready for the deep end of my prayers?

What I Mean Is...

Are you frequently explaining yourself and your ideas over and over to the same people? It can be frustrating when you feel like nobody gets you and what you're about. Our desire to be heard and understood is our hunger for significance in this lifetime.

You are significant. You are heard. And you are seen completely by your Creator. Your hunger is very real, and it is also a blessing. It will draw you to God. It will lead you to seek fulfillment and identity in his grace.

God, it's a great security and comfort to speak to you from my heart and be heard. You don't dismiss me. You don't see my struggles as minor even though they don't compare with those of many of your children. What I mean is...thank you for loving me.

Today Is Sacred

You can go on a pilgrimage to a far-off land to understand the sacred. You can practice traditions that honor what is holy. But the sacred is even more accessible. You can experience it through daily living. We make the pursuit of holiness too complicated. We introduce conflict and drama where there's supposed to be simplicity and peace.

Your life is sacred. There's nothing ordinary or trivial about who you are and what you do. Center your life in God's peace, and live with full awareness of God's love. When you celebrate the privilege of being alive and knowing God, you're savoring the sacred.

I've traveled far emotionally. This journey of trial and doubt was not required by you, yet somehow it felt necessary for my own understanding of faith. Help me to hold on to your love wherever I am. I wish to carry the sacred with me from this point onward.

Abundance

Words of Abundance

Let my teaching fall like rain
and my words descend like dew,
like showers on new grass,
like abundant rain on tender plants.

Deuteronomy 32:2

You anoint my head with oil;
my cup overflows. Surely goodness and love
will follow me all the days of my life,
and I will dwell in the house of the Lord forever.

Psalm 23:5-6

They will tell of the power of your awesome
works, and I will proclaim your great deeds.
They will celebrate your abundant goodness
and joyfully sing of your righteousness.

Psalm 145:6-7

He will also send you rain for the seed you
sow in the ground, and the food that comes
from the land will be rich and plentiful.

Isaiah 30:23

I will bring health and healing to [this city];
I will heal my people and will let them
enjoy abundant peace and security.

JEREMIAH 33:6

You will have plenty to eat, until you are full,
and you will praise the name
of the LORD your God,
who has worked wonders for you;
never again will my people be shamed.

JOEL 2:26

From the fullness of his grace we have all
received one blessing after another.

JOHN 1:16

In union with Christ you have become rich in all
things, including all speech and all knowledge.

1 CORINTHIANS 1:5 TEV

God did not give us a spirit of timidity, but a
spirit of power, of love and of self-discipline.

2 TIMOTHY 1:7

Affluence or Influence

I don't know which income-level box you check on your tax forms. I don't know if you own a vacation home or rent a one-bedroom apartment. But I know that you're wealthy with influence. You might not realize it yet, but the deeper you grow in your faith and the more you rely on God's strength…the greater influence you'll have in the lives of others.

Don't hold back from sharing or expressing your faith. You've been blessed with abundance. Give to the poor in spirit. Give to those who need God. Spread the wealth.

My personal influence wouldn't be much…but my influence through my faith and understanding of you is significant. You change lives, God. I know this deeply from my own experience. May I not hold back my wealth of belief from those who are hungry.

Laughter

Do you get enough laughter in your life? What brings you to giggles? What—are you too mature for that? Are you too poised or proper? Taste God's delight in life. He wants you to experience the depths of meaning and ministry, but he also calls you to savor the gift of your time with others and your time walking with him on this earth.

Turn up the joy in your day. Consider adding more music, a comedy movie, stories that celebrate life, and moments when you have absolutely nothing planned except to ponder something funny. Lift up an offering of a joyful heart.

I'll approach today with a cranked-up level of joy. I want to be free of whatever holds me back from extending smiles and helpful gestures. Open my eyes to the joy that's all around me.

Having It All

The debate about whether women can have it all will always be hot. Each of us holds on to versions of what our "all" looks like. The hard truth is that there are always choices and sacrifices to be made. The sweet truth is that when we choose to have faith in the sacrifice that Christ made, we do have it all.

Spiritual abundance isn't something we earn, plan for, coordinate, or schedule in our lives. It's a gift. And it's all yours.

I had a warped version of "having it all" until
I came to you with nothing but my broken
heart, my sin, and my hunger. Everything looks
different now. There isn't a level to achieve, there's
a God to adore. This truly is having it all.

Plenty

The cornucopia was a symbol of food and abundance in the fifth century B.C. Yet most of us only learned about it in grade school at Thanksgiving. As a fifth grader, my version of food abundance would've been a stash of Junior Mints! But, we heard that abundance was a cornucopia, a horn-shaped woven basket overflowing with fruits and vegetables.

Do you question whether there's abundance in your life? Do you ask God for sweets when he's provided you with a bounty of vegetables? Consider what you're longing for, and compare it to God's best for you. There's a good chance you're standing in the land of plenty right now. Accept the offering of your good life…and remember to give thanks.

I have more than I need. I have more than I'm able to keep track of. May I only have desires for whatever you want me to take hold of, God. Thank you for this bountiful life.

Toss a Title

Women! We have such simple goals—we want to be healers, givers, mothers, wives, best friends, contributors, leaders, mediators, protectors, shepherds, moderators, controllers, caregivers, helpmates, teachers, servants, designers, contractors…did I leave any of your favorites off the list?

Some roles are assigned to us (without our even realizing it), others we step into eagerly, and still more we take on because we're trying to become something we aren't. Review your list of job titles; ask God which ones are intended for you. Delegate or toss the rest. Living the abundant life sometimes requires that we get rid of a few things first.

Am I wearing a hat that doesn't even belong to me? I tend to take over things before I ask you if they fit into my purpose. It's time to delegate, relinquish control, and give more of myself to the roles you choose for me.

Love's Mark

What marks your speech, your walk, your interaction with strangers, your work, your patience with family? Observe yourself for a day, a week, or longer. See if there's proof of your faith and your personal journey with God. Are you inclined toward joy, compassion, conscientiousness, kindness, and authenticity? Or do you bury these evidences of belief beneath your scars of the past and symbols of worldly success?

God's love leaves an impression in the material of your soul. Let this be the mark of your identity and value.

Is there proof of your hand on my life? Do I speak and act differently because I know and love the God of sea and sky? May my life be marked by my love for you.

Made for More

I sometimes catch myself stopping short of giving my all. I know when I'm living only a portion of the life God intends for me, because I feel that burden of loss and dissatisfaction. My pride and my worry and my track record all rise up to create a barrier between where I stop and the far-reaching life God is guiding me toward.

When you call out to God because you crave more meaning and significance, he'll ask you to examine your heart and your actions. What barriers separate you from a faith of substance? Make the choice to give your all so that you can receive *his* all for your life.

When I hold back, please nudge me forward so that I'll express who I am and what I'm feeling. I've missed too many opportunities because I was scared and reluctant to trust you. Free me from this worry.

Second Helpings

It's hard to refuse second helpings. The next spoonful is as tantalizing as the first. We don't want to refuse the continuation of pleasure, even if the second helpings add up to undesired love handles. Just as your mind overrides your physical fullness and says yes to that next slice of cake, your spirit can override your mind.

When you surrender to what is best for your life, you can appreciate the blessing of the first serving without having to indulge in the next offering. You can savor what you have rather than mourning what you don't. Replace misleading hungers with second helpings of contentment and peace of mind.

It all looks so good. I do want more than I can handle, more than any one person should have, and certainly more than I need. Help me learn to hunger only for what is of you.

Goldilocks

Do you try out people, jobs, dreams, and even your faith to see if it suits your fancy? We've learned to evaluate all of our choices. That's responsible, right? But this overdeveloped desire to get the perfect deal, relationship, or path of faith can keep you from experiencing the joy of everyday moments. Real living and real faith happen in the trenches, not just on the mountaintop.

I believe that sometimes God is merely asking us to commit to where we're at, so that he can work on us. And so he can show us how he turns ordinary living into extraordinary living. Commit your days to God, and commit to stepping into your life with hope.

Why is it so hard to stand firm in my life as it is? While I grab on to one thing, I'm always looking past it to see what else might come my way. Help me focus on the work you're doing in me and in my life right now. Don't let me throw that away.

A Woman's Strength

It takes a lot of emotional strength to be a woman. The pressures can be great. We press on through pain, through adversity, through change, through times when life isn't all we had hoped for *and* when life is more than we'd hoped and we're struggling to keep up!

Your true strength is discovered when you rely on God's vision and love. Even if—especially if—you've never been able to rely on anyone, give yourself over to the abundance of God's care. You won't believe how good it feels to be wrapped in endless support.

Support groups are great, but they have nothing on you, God. I can come to you at any time and for any help I need. I'm slow to ask for help, but I'm getting better at it. Embrace me. I want to feel the protection and strength of my Savior.

Contentment

Words of Contentment

On that day they offered great sacrifices, rejoicing
because God had given them great joy. The
women and children also rejoiced. The sound of
rejoicing in Jerusalem could be heard far away.

NEHEMIAH 12:43

If they obey and serve him,
they will spend the rest of their days in prosperity
and their years in contentment.

JOB 36:11

The precepts of the LORD are right,
giving joy to the heart.
The commands of the LORD are radiant,
giving light to the eyes.

PSALM 19:8

Show me your ways, O LORD,
teach me your paths;
guide me in your truth and teach me,
for you are God my Savior,
and my hope is in you all day long.

PSALM 25:4-5

Satisfy us in the morning with your unfailing love,
that we may sing for joy and be glad all our days.

PSALM 90:14

A man can do nothing better than to eat
and drink and find satisfaction in his work.
This too, I see, is from the hand of God, for
without him, who can eat or find enjoyment?

ECCLESIASTES 2:24-25

I know what it is to be in need, and I know
what it is to have plenty. I have learned the
secret of being content in any and every
situation, whether well fed or hungry, whether
living in plenty or in want. I can do everything
through him who gives me strength.

PHILIPPIANS 4:12-13

Godliness with contentment is great gain. For
we brought nothing into the world, and we
can take nothing out of it. But if we have food
and clothing, we will be content with that.

1 TIMOTHY 6:6-8

Rise Up or Settle Down

What were you doing when you were told to settle down as a child? Clapping during a hymn at church? Playing spoons at the restaurant? Savoring candy (loudly) at a sibling's recital? As an adult, now you get to decide whether you want to settle down. I don't mean the "get married, have kids" settling down, I mean the "act a certain way" mandate.

Don't edit out the moments of happiness and creativity. When you feel the urge to laugh or the inclination to sing along to a favorite song, let it out! Give your spirit of joy a chance to express itself!

I want to express myself and my happiness. Why do I always temper my joy with a dose of maturity and proper behavior? I've held back from delighting in your wonder for too long. I'll let the joy you give me rise up as I sing praises to you and to this life.

Wellspring

When joy rises to the surface of your emotions, do you let it change your mood, your experience, your sense of possibility? Or do you hold it back for some reason? Maybe you've been hurt when you let your guard down? Or maybe there are so many concerns and trials to consider that joy seems an improper use of time and energy and self.

Real happiness, pure joy, is never a waste. And it can never be used up. God's heart is our wellspring of joy. When a wave of delight comes over you, let it sweep you into his presence. Let the curious wonder of joy draw you to a life rich with blessings.

I'm relatively happy. But I've noticed that this happiness doesn't necessarily impact my daily perspective as it should. Why doesn't it influence the way I treat others and the way I respond to your leading? I'm not going to hold back anymore.

Sliding Toward Yes

Do you recognize this loop of thought: *I don't think so. That probably won't work. I'd rather not. What if something bad happens? Why bother at all? Not this time. No. Absolutely not.* Ah, the slippery slope of no. It begins with doubt and slides on into full negativity. Have you been on this ride?

Consider taking a similar ride, but one that is redirected by faith's possibility: *I might. That could work. I'll think about it. This could really work. Why not? This timing is perfect. Yes. Absolutely!*

Stop me when my thoughts start to spiral downward. I have your sweet mercy and endless grace, and yet I dwell on the negative blips or my projected fears during the day. Help me to set my mind on things from above so that my spirit and mood soar.

First Impression

Days when I wake up motivated and ready for my tasks are good days. A sense of anticipation comes over me, and I feel…happy. Glad. Hopeful. But other mornings I wake up with a slight tremor of dread or restlessness. There might be a huge deadline or an uncomfortable conversation slated for the day. Or I just feel "off."

Too often we let our first impression—our wake-up mood—dictate the rest of the day. Contentment comes when we give over those initial bits of dread, fear, reluctance, or even laziness to God. Consider it a morning offering. Release these to God so he can shape them into something useful. Turn first impressions into expressions of faith.

I think I'll be giving my first impressions to you a lot in the near future. I need a retraining of my heart and mind. Let my first thoughts be of thankfulness and my first words be of praise to you.

Mimic God's Words

Conversations with others can lift your spirit. But your inner dialogue can go downhill when you meet with negative people. It's vital to spiritually prepare yourself for these conversations. Before you start to mimic the neighbor, friend, or coworker who laments every turn of life, focus on words of God to turn your heart upward.

Consider Philippians 4:8: "Finally, brothers, whatever is true, whatever is noble, whatever is right, whatever is pure, whatever is lovely, whatever is admirable—if anything is excellent or praiseworthy—think about such things." And speak of such things!

My own routine...my monologue...has become very worldly and even negative. How did the words I focus on become these words of destruction? I will release those and turn to the words of Philippians—words that give life and faith.

Come On, Get Happy

Did you grow up in a home that was nurturing, joyful, and creative? Or did you have to figure out a way to happiness on your own? Some of us take a long time to experience happiness. The certainty of God's unconditional love provides us with a current of contentment. But happiness requires a nudge now and then.

I nudge by listening to music or buying fresh pads of sketch paper and new pens. Maybe you finger-paint. Bake and decorate cookies. Build a sandcastle. Plan a trip. Read a romance novel. Get goofy with your child. Eat an entire coconut cream pie. Simple pleasures cultivate a heart of happiness!

Joy to the world! You came to save us all. The world is beyond beautiful. I can't stop staring at the moon. And I love the taste of a good nectarine. Oh, Lord...remind me to celebrate all these blessings.

On Your Way

Where are you off to? You look so busy. Can I say it? You even look a bit harried. I get that way sometimes. Have you ever caught yourself holding your breath for long stretches of time? I've done that! No wonder we get anxious or suddenly lose steam and all sense of direction.

Did you just step over this moment to get to the next one? What's your hurry? There will never be another today like today. Give yourself time to breathe. While you're on your way to great things, you might be missing the greatest thing of all—your life!

I've hurdled more than a few moments to think ahead about my job or my agenda. I feel compelled to because life and family become overwhelming. God, turn my attention to the present so that I can honor each day you give me.

Savoring Satisfaction

When is enough really enough? Are you satisfied with your purchase of a great skirt…or do you immediately want to buy two more just like it in different colors? Have you moved into a bigger home and then wished for something with more amenities? Did you take your dream vacation that wasn't nearly as good as you imagined it?

You'll miss out on a lot of living if you're never satisfied. The power of "want" always overrides the truth and beauty of your experience. Practice the art of satisfaction. Start building up your daily life by embracing it, seeing the good, and celebrating each gift of goodness that comes your way.

My wants sneak up on me, God. I'll barely think of them, and then an opportunity to satisfy them arises and I'm obsessed. Mostly I want material luxuries, not necessities. Give me a pure heart that longs for wholeness, not the emptiness of wanting.

Look Carefully

Examine your life as it is, not as you want it to be or as someone else tells you it should be. Contentment comes when we face the day before us without pretense or lies and own up to who we are. There are so many ways to shape today and to turn toward goodness, delight, and purpose.

Your decisions will be wiser, your hope brighter, and your steps more sure when you remove the rose-colored glasses and see the brilliant colors of a real life—the life God has for you. Look closely; it's breathtaking.

This is a kaleidoscope life you have given me. I don't want to settle for a fake image of what life is about. I want it all...the brilliant colors of sadness, hope, uncertainty, and peace. My contentment becomes brighter the more I rest with your faithfulness.

The Contents of a Life

What fills your life? Do you gather friends together often? Do your children make you smile and fuel your purpose? Does work reward with feelings of accomplishment and perseverance? Does your commitment to exercise leave you energetic and happy?

A life of contentment comes from the good, lovely, substantial contents of your life. Are the things you believe in evident through your actions, words, and choices? Gather in your heart all the hope, compassion, integrity, faith, and kindness it can hold—these are the roots of your contentment.

I don't always fill up with things and thoughts that are pleasing to you. I can go the way of selfish or fearful too often. I want the contents of my heart to be the hope of your love and the endless supply of peace you give to those who come to you.

Intentional
Living

Words of Intentional Living

In your unfailing love you will lead
the people you have redeemed.

EXODUS 15:13

Walk in all the way that the LORD your
God has commanded you, so that you
may live and prosper and prolong your
days in the land that you will possess.

DEUTERONOMY 5:33

May the words of my mouth and the meditation
of my heart be pleasing in your sight,
O LORD, my Rock and my Redeemer.

PSALM 19:14

You will become wise,
and your knowledge will give you pleasure.
Your insight and understanding will protect you
and prevent you from doing the wrong thing.

PROVERBS 2:10-12 TEV

Whenever you possibly can,
do good to those who need it. Never tell your
neighbors to wait until tomorrow
if you can help him now.

Proverbs 3:27-28 tev

~~~

Whatever your hand finds to do, do it with
all your might, for in the grave, where you
are going, there is neither working nor
planning nor knowledge nor wisdom.

Ecclesiastes 9:10

~~~

No good tree bears bad fruit, nor does
a bad tree bear good fruit. Each tree
is recognized by its own fruit.

Luke 6:43-44

~~~

Always give yourselves fully to the work
of the Lord, because you know that your
labor in the Lord is not in vain.

1 Corinthians 15:58

Drawing Straws

Let's see, which to choose. They all look about the same. If you choose the long one, you'll surely get what you want out of the situation. If you are sadly a bad guesser and select the stubby one, you're destined to fall short of your goals. You're doomed. No pressure, now choose.

Okay, you probably don't draw straws to decide whom to marry, which job to take, or where to invest your money. Yet, is your system any more spiritually valid? Do you pray over concerns? Do you take your pending decisions to God's Word? Don't leave your life up to chance—give it over to God; he'll draw you closer to his wisdom.

I've gambled away too many choices because I approached them without your wisdom. No more. I want you to know exactly what is going on in my life, and I want to base my decisions on the certainty of your leading. I won't leave the state of my faith to chance.

Willing and Able

Can't. Won't. Which is your word of choice when concocting a reason to not do something? I use them both interchangeably and incorrectly myself. There are likely some very appropriate times to use either word. But *can't* often means you're afraid to try. *Won't* frequently implies fear, pride, or stubbornness.

When you select either word as your "get out of jail free" card, you could be missing out on opportunities to grow, rely on God, discover your gifting, trust others, become more fulfilled, and thrive. That's a lot to give up. A life without excuses becomes a life of purpose. Are you willing?

God, reveal to me why I hesitate so often to follow through. I know there is much fear in me, but why haven't I given my repeat worries to you? My grip on them is fierce. I need your strength to let go of my excuses.

Alive in the World

There's a difference between living and being alive! When you're just living, you ask God to help you survive the day or to have enough energy to appear put together. When you're alive, you feel it to your core. You awaken to God's leading in your heart and soul and through the desires, pursuits, and longings he is giving to you.

When you're alive, you're present for what God is doing in your life and through your life. You clearly hear his whisper of encouragement, and you respond with a "yes, I'll follow!"

When will I understand how truly precious it is to be alive? I have meaningful moments with my family that remind me, but then forget when I'm shopping, driving, talking, planning, or complaining. Show me what being alive in you is all about.

Divine Awareness

Have you ever reached a Saturday and wondered how you got there? What happened to Tuesday? Did that project get done on Wednesday? When life becomes a blur, make a commitment to slow down. (I'd recommend stopping, but you'd probably ignore me.) Pray for God's perspective for your day. Assign value to each and every moment.

We think time flies, but really we're flying through time, propelled by our false sense of urgency. Are worries about next week's meeting crowding out your prayer time? Is your five-year plan more important than the conversation you're having with a friend in need right now? Deliberate living gives you divine awareness.

Give my life focus, Lord. When I set my gaze upon you and your purpose for me, I can see the steps before me. I can clearly distinguish what is of you from what is of the world or my personal desires. Help me be deliberate in all I do.

Knockin'

When opportunity knocks, and before you respond and move forward, check your motives to be sure they are right and pure. Is this possibility about self-gain or true purpose? Does it follow God's leading in your life? Does it fit with the other decisions you have already made with prayerful consideration?

Seek God's wisdom and direction, and ask whether you're being led by a pure heart. "Knock and the door will be opened to you. For everyone who asks receives; he who seeks finds; and to him who knocks, the door will be opened" (Matthew 7:7-8). Before you respond to the latest opportunity, do some knocking of your own.

Are you leading me today, God? I've felt a pull for some time now in a certain direction, but I want to be sure it is from you. I seek your wisdom and then your peace so that I can know this is the way to go. Thank you for always answering.

Instant Messaging God

During the day, we send up little messages to God. Some are mutterings. Some are quick calls for patience, compassion, perspective. Some are general "Lord, help me" cries. While these one-sided conversations don't make for a deep exchange with God, they can lead like stepping stones to a greater prayer life.

Your spontaneous petitions and praises reflect a dependence on God that will lead to a more personal, intimate relationship with him. Follow them to times of focused dialogue with the Creator...after all, this two-sided conversation is life-changing!

I talk a lot at you, God, but I don't always pay attention to your response. Forgive me for the times when all I can do is blurt out my needs and problems. I pray to have my random petitions become a real dialogue with you. Do you have a minute? I want to really talk.

Leave Them Behind

At first, expectations can seem like motivation. The sheer force of their existence can drive you forward in your career, personal goals, relationships, and dreams. But if you rely on expectations for fuel, you'll eventually be disappointed. They offer only the illusion of power and strength.

When you stop living to fulfill expectations and start living to be filled by God's promises, you'll experience the difference. Where there was guilt, you'll have grace. Where there was pressure, you'll have faith. Where there was a shove to succeed, there will be a leading toward purpose.

So many people lay claim to my time and my efforts. These expectations define my life more than my faith at times. I want to be discerning so that I'm following your leading rather than running from pressures.

Resisting Rest

I'm so stubborn, it's amazing I became a person of faith. I am reluctant to ask for help. A friend knew I was going to move a big piece of furniture, and she said, "Please tell me you'll get someone to help you." I smiled and promptly went home and moved it myself. It took a long time, I was sore the next two days, but I did it.

Do you wear your independence like a badge of honor? Do you resist resting in God's strength, the help of another, or even the compassion of friends? Don't go it alone. That burden you're staring at, sizing up, and plotting against on your own is meant to be shared. And you know exactly who to ask for help.

I need your help. There, I said it. I'm very independent. You know that about me. But you also see the ridiculous things I try to do all by myself. It isn't a sign of strength to resist your peace and your help. Forgive me for trying to be my own provider and savior.

Sound Tracks

I settled into my favorite chair with my favorite beverage at my favorite coffee shop—ready for an enjoyable round of reading. But for some reason I had no focus. Then I noticed the frenzied, classical music playing overhead. The music's spiraling intensity undermined my best intentions to concentrate.

What is the distracting or destructive background noise in your life? The relentless criticism of a parent, a boss, or your own mind? The loud rattle of past mistakes trailing behind you? The grating of someone else's negativity? Tune in to God's voice and his calling. It's the intended sound track for your life. It drowns out the chaos and leads you with a rhythm that soothes the soul.

I tune in to words that do not uplift me. I let my heart's beating match the rhythm of the world. Change my sound track, Lord. I want to start humming to your hope and tapping my toes to your timing. You're my new song, and I will sing it boldly.

Tithing Time

Pie charts make for great business presentations. Each segment of the circle represents a portion of the total element being measured—income, population, whatever. In an instant, the presenter can make her point with a visual representation of often intangible elements. If you generated a "my distribution of time" chart, what would your portion spent with God or *for* God look like?

If you're eating humble pie about now, start increasing the size of that slice of your pie chart destined for prayer and devotion. Go from a sliver to a wedge. Redistribute the intangible of time so time for God becomes a significant part of your day.

I'd like to say that everything I do and experience is done with you and for you, God. But that wouldn't be close to true. I have good intentions, but my pure offerings to you are a slim slice of my days. I will work to increase this portion, Lord.

Dreams and Aspirations

Words of Aspiration

Commit your way to the Lord; trust in
him and he will do this: He will make your
righteousness shine like the dawn, the justice
of your cause like the noonday sun.

Psalm 37:5-6

Ｃ

The Lord will fulfill [his purpose] for me;
your love, O Lord, endures forever—
do not abandon the works of your hands.

Psalm 138:8

Ｃ

A longing fulfilled is sweet to the soul.

Proverbs 13:19

Ｃ

There is surely a future hope for you,
and your hope will not be cut off.

Proverbs 23:18

Ｃ

Just as honey from the comb is sweet
on your tongue, you may be sure that
wisdom is good for the soul. Get wisdom
and you have a bright future.

Proverbs 24:13-14 TEV

I alone know the plans I have for you, plans to bring you prosperity and not disaster, plans to bring about the future you hope for. Then you will call to me. You will come and pray to me, and I will answer you. You will seek me, and you will find me because you will seek me with all your heart.

JEREMIAH 29:11-13 TEV

Just as you excel in everything—in faith, in speech, in knowledge, in complete earnestness and in your love for us—see that you also excel in this grace of giving.

2 CORINTHIANS 8:7

Let us hold unswervingly to the hope we profess, for he who promised is faithful. And let us consider how we may spur one another on toward love and good deeds.

HEBREWS 10:23-24

Birthing Plan

The moment a new idea, a dream, or a brilliant goal is conceived is a wonderful thing. You get chills of anticipation. Your imagination leaps to how great life will be when this dream is fulfilled. But then days later, the thrill fades. By the next month you've almost forgotten the lovely goal.

If you want to give birth to a dream, you need a birthing plan! Ask God for the next step. Seek his validation and the support of others. Figure out which of your gifts will have to be honed. Pray each step of the way, and be open to the answers. You never know when God's plan will lead you toward an even bigger dream than the one you conceived.

Help me give birth to this dream, God. What is my next move? Hold me back when I'm supposed to wait. Give me discernment so that I can see where you are leading me. Help me to let go of any dream that is solely of my own making.

Life in 360

I don't always glean what I'm supposed to learn from life situations. My eyes are on the prize of finishing. I'm determined to meet deadlines. I'm motivated by pressure. I'm driven to finish project A so I can move on to project B. Only lately am I realizing how limited my vision of life is.

It's good to have focus. To finish what you start—as long as you don't hurry forth with blinders on. There's so much life happening around you. There are people in need. Doors open for you to walk through. And there's inspiration when you look to the left or the right of the horizon's center. Life in 360 degrees has a beautiful view.

Expand my view, God. I want to take all of life in. When my focus is on my stuff, I miss out on seeing the people in my life, the joy, and the path you present. It will be a lot for me to take in—this new view—but I'm excited.

I Always Thought…

When you gather with friends and the conversation stalls on the mundane activities like laundry, deadlines, carpooling, do you ever stare off into the distance and say, "I always thought life would be different"? When left to your own thoughts, do you dwell on the pursuit that never went anywhere? The idea that never took flight? The relationship that never evolved beyond friendship?

If you give what hasn't happened more importance than what *is* happening, you'll miss the dream God's planting today. And you won't notice the ones he's already fulfilled!

Sometimes I get trapped in the ordinary. I don't want to be a "what if" woman. I want to notice all that you're doing and have done. With this awareness, I can walk with conviction and fearlessness.

Dream a Little Dream

Are you so caught up in today's pressures that you forget to give attention to your hopes? Your dreams? I know. We're all so very practical. There's so much to do today that it's difficult to invest in those dreams. But believe me, they need a bit of your attention. Keep your dreams alive with prayer, time spent reflecting on your goals, and also time spent journaling or pondering the possibilities of your life.

God gives you longings and hopes. Don't let agendas, pressures, and expectations drown out those seeds of your purpose and direction. Dream a little dream.

A little space would do me wonders. I need space in my life, my schedule, and my thought life so that I can think on and pray over all the dreams you give me. You inspire me daily and give me great hope for a future.

Pursuits of a Life

Investment of self, time, money, and ability can meld together and become the launching pad for the life God has for you. Where do you invest your self, money, and ability right now? Do you seek opportunities that are of God? That feel like your calling? That feed your soul? That seem tied to purpose?

The pursuits of your life do matter. They reflect your priorities. They're born of your heart, and they reveal your calling. Redirect your steps today if they do not lead to God's purpose. Take in the wonders and delights that the Creator has orchestrated on your behalf. Celebrate with each step.

Step one. Step two. Step three. These are all mapped out by you and for me. It's incredible. I want to sit with this amazing truth. This time I'm making room for the wonder of it all.

Creator in Action

Inspiration is always such a sweet surprise. Do you get that rush of creativity, thoughts with power and ingenuity behind them, or the pull toward something fresh and wonderful? These great, and somewhat rare, experiences let us peek into the Creator's workshop. We get a glimpse of how God lovingly and joyfully forms miracles.

Give the work of your life over to the Master. He'll blow away the dust, he'll rub out the rough spots, he'll treat it like a brilliant treasure. He'll model the profound love he has for the heart he shaped in you.

My inspiration comes from you. When I feel the incredible joy of an idea coming on, I know it's a gift from your heart to mine. I want to offer it back to you so that you can shape it, smooth it, and refine it into something worthy.

Give Yourself Up

Each of us has a unique voice, gifting, and perspective to contribute. You admire strength and ability in your neighbor, your friend, or your child—but do you recognize such worth in yourself? God does. He sees your very core. His vision encompasses not just what you've done, but all that you're made to accomplish through him.

Don't hold back from contributing who you are and what you have to give. It's too great of a loss for the world to bear. Release your inclination to align your identity with your mistakes, and behold your beauty and value as a new creation in God's grace.

Why do I sell myself short when you have created me, held me close, and breathed life into my spirit? You call me to be a servant, but you don't tell me that what I have to offer is less than that of another. Teach me the balance, Lord. I know I have a lot to give.

Crystal Ball

We might not seek advice from a crystal sphere or from staring at the stars, but we occasionally, foolishly look to things other than God for a vision of what's to come. The amazing part of being a woman of belief is that we know what the future holds. We don't have specific images, numbers, figures, and details, but we have direction and promises.

When you need a glimpse of somewhere to place your hope, look to God. He'll show you exactly what today, tomorrow, and forever holds for you, his child.

*What will happen? What will my life be like?
Will my children be well and good? What changes
will take place soon? As much as I want to know
all of this...all that I need to know is that I can
always turn to you, and you will never leave me.*

See Yourself

When you look at your family and friends, do you see their gifts so clearly? It's easy to encourage them because their talents shine and their strengths are so evident; meanwhile you are reluctant to accept a compliment. Are you willing to cast yourself in a good light? Do you believe in the purpose and plan God has mapped on your heart?

Today is a chance to claim and honor all that's wonderful in you. Express your gifts. Truly see your intelligence, personality, and uniqueness—they are part of you, and they are evidence of your Maker.

*Lord, what do you see when you look at me? I
see the times I let others down. I see the wounds
that remain open because I refuse to forgive. I see
mistake after mistake. Let me see what you see.
I need to see my life in the light of your love.*

Am I There Yet?

Is this life I'm living really my purpose? Did I miss a turn somewhere? Do you ever scratch your head and wonder such things? Doubts won't destroy dreams, but they certainly can delay them. If you stand before God and play twenty questions, ask for confirmation, direction, and answers.

God doesn't give us hope and then sit back to watch us flounder. He's with us every step of the way; he's leading, he's holding back, and he's carrying us. And when you journey with God—you *are* there, exactly where you're supposed to be.

Sorry for all the questions, but they fill my head, and I have to get them out. Sometimes they lead me astray, away from what you have planned for me. Can my questions be an offering today? May this be my prayer of need, dependence, and trust in your presence.

Hope

Words of Hope

Who cuts a channel for the torrents of rain,
and a path for the thunderstorm,
to water a land where no man lives,
a desert with no one in it,
to satisfy a desolate wasteland and
make it sprout with grass?

JOB 38:25-27

You turned my wailing into dancing; you removed
my sackcloth and clothed me with joy, that my
heart may sing to you and not be silent.
O LORD my God, I will give you thanks forever.

PSALM 30:11-12

Since you are my rock and my fortress,
for the sake of your name lead and guide me.

PSALM 31:3

Teach me to do your will,
for you are my God;
may your good Spirit
lead me on level ground.

PSALM 143:10

You were wearied by all your ways,
but you would not say, "It is hopeless."
You found renewal of your strength,
and so you did not faint.

ISAIAH 57:10

Jesus answered, "Those who drink this water will
get thirsty again, but those who drink the water
that I will give them will never be thirsty again.
The water that I will give them will become in
them a spring which will provide them with
life-giving water and give them eternal life."

JOHN 4:13-14 TEV

Just as the sufferings of Christ flow over into
our lives, so also through Christ our comfort
overflows. If we are distressed, it is for your
comfort and salvation; if we are comforted, it is
for your comfort, which produces in you patient
endurance of the same sufferings we suffer.

2 CORINTHIANS 1:5-6

Breaking the Ice

Ice fishing. That's not a topic you ponder every day. The extreme cold combined with the need for great patience would send me running for the nearest sunny beach. Yet there's something noble in this sport. The fishermen cut a hole in the desolate surface of nature's terrain and tap into water teeming with life below. It's an act of hope.

Our daily horizon can become an expanse of white noise, cold encounters, and frozen emotions. But if we break the surface of nominal living with prayer and commitment to the things of God, we'll see that our hearts are teeming with life and purpose. It is then that we can cast our line in the waters of hope.

*I have been frozen. Locked into a pattern of activity,
going through my days without prayer and without
considering the deeper purpose of my waking life.
God, help me to break through the surface so that
I reach into my soul to your living waters.*

Tower of Fear

When my fear of a situation or outcome becomes great, I use absolute terms like "all or nothing," "always," and "never." I predict fear-based scenarios: It will be a disaster. Nobody will like me. I'll fail. Others always fail me. This builds and builds. When I come down from my tower of fear, I'm dizzy from the swift shift in altitude.

What escalating worries, anxieties, and doubts build up so quickly that before you know it, you're standing miles above reality on a very weak platform of lies and deceptions? Come down from the tower. Better yet, stay tethered to God's truth, love, and wisdom before you start the climb.

I put up such walls with my absolutes based on fear. God, give me a spirit of peace and humility. Only when I give each fear over to you as it arises will the tower of my insecurities tumble.

Mercy, Mercy Me

Are troubled skies forming? Are dark clouds covering your life? It can be a lonely experience to prepare for a personal storm. Maybe those you depend on most are the ones causing the earth to shake beneath you. Are the wild winds of fear, anxiety, or sorrow gathering inside of you?

When the sky does open up and the first drops fall, there's shelter for you in the arms of God. He will carry you through this. He will protect you from what brews in your heart and what blows across the landscape of life as you know it. There is no trial or trouble, sin or sadness, defeat or depression that will keep you from God's sweet mercy.

I've been through this storm before, but when the winds start, it always sends me trembling. I struggle through the same problems and doubts to get back to faith. Why do I make it so hard? You're right here with me, Lord.

Come So Far

Visit your personal scrapbook. Where have you been, and who were you? What has God done in your life and through your obedience? How did he make something you tried to tear apart into something whole and useful? Are there parts of your life that never made sense until God put the pieces back together in a new way?

Sadly, we often equate mistakes with absolute failure... as though redemption didn't exist. You've come so far—and not as a result of random collisions of right time/right place. Recognize the journey and be grateful for it—God has brought you here.

Only you have brought me here. Only your love has carried me through the trenches of difficulty. Only your mercy has covered me. Only your intervention has saved me. Only your grace has redeemed me.

Light Your Way

The look of the sun rising over a field of wheat is much different than the view of morning's first light over the white slopes of a mountain. Your experience of God's light cast across your life changes with the scenery of your journey.

When the terrain of your day is rough, God's light is a warm glow. When life soars smoothly, there are bright rays of joy. When you're stumbling along the cliffs of trial, his love is a lighthouse's beam, directing you home. No matter what you're experiencing, God's hope radiates across the landscape of your life.

When I'm cast in darkness I need only to look for your light. It's my focal point and my beacon. Lead me home, Lord.

Matter of Convenience

Those 24/7 corner markets are fabulous. I can go there for potato chips during a late night of work. When I want to perk up midafternoon, I can go get a cup of coffee. And on those days when I wake up at dawn, I can walk to the market, get a donut, and have a brief exchange with someone else who is alert at that ridiculous hour.

God's hope is available to us 24 hours a day. Pursue it when you need comfort. Go to it when you need a pick-me-up. Ask for it when you feel alone in the universe. Hope is not elusive or a great mystery. It always exists. And it is available right when you need it.

Sometimes I wander in circles looking for acceptance and connection. Your embrace is open to take me in, reassure me, and lead me toward your purpose for my life. My aimlessness turns toward direction and hope.

Open to Love

Lost love and broken promises can sever our ability to hope for the best. We might say we want to heal, yet most of us describe the times we've been hurt with sadness or anger that is fresh, raw, and very close to the surface. Are you nurturing your pain more than your hope?

When you give your wounds to God's healing mercy, he'll expand your heart to make room for hope, faith, and new experiences. He'll restore your openness to love.

I've been nursing these long-endured emotional injuries with all the wrong remedies. I want to experience complete restoration. Please separate me from my pain. You remind me that I'm your child. I don't want my wounds to be my identity ever again.

His Embrace

As much as we might wish for it, our everyday faith doesn't always have the intimacy of a one-on-one chat with God in our living rooms. There are times when God seems far away. He isn't absent...nevertheless, when that sense of distance rises up, it can throw us for a loop. It can send some on a journey of struggle.

If you're facing a time of distance or silence, rest in the knowledge of God's presence. Stand on the security of his faithfulness. Start a conversation with God, like you would with a best friend, and allow the dialogue to unfold. God is there. Your hope will remind you of his everpresent embrace.

When there is silence, Lord, help me to seek the solace of your Word and of your peace. These, too, are here to guide me and bring me comfort and show me the workings of faith—even during troubled times. May my earnest prayers reach you always.

Life Adjustment

The world's version of hope might consist of an attitude adjustment, but faith's version of hope adjusts everything. Here are ways you can get hope to take on dimension in daily living: Let it infuse your speech with uplifting, generous, and positive words. Come at your trials and problems from a wide angle that makes room for possibility. Start your day knowing that up ahead there will be good conversations, interactions, decisions, and chances to reach out.

There are many ways for hope to be manifested in your life.

God, I want to be hope filled. Give me your eyes for every situation. Give me your heart for others, my family, and my own life. Refresh my sense of possibility so that I anticipate good things.

Is It Any Wonder?

When in the presence of children, it's fun to play make-believe. You can create a kingdom right in your living room. You can play catch with the moon. You can string stars onto a necklace. You can turn into a dove and soar to heaven.

Hope isn't fantasy, but it holds the same promise as time spent pretending the utterly impossible is completely possible. Hope isn't hiding from real life; it's embracing the realness of God. And about those fruit of the imagination listed above...God can do them all. Is it any wonder he makes belief out of a sprinkle of hope?

*Nothing is impossible for you! You aren't a magician;
you're the Maker of all I see and know...and all I
don't see and don't know. My far-reaching imagination
can never surpass the wonders of your real power.*

Wholeness

Words of Wholeness

You, O Lord, are always my shield from danger;
you give me victory and restore my courage.

PSALM 3:3 TEV

＊

As a father is kind to his children,
so the Lord is kind to those who honor him.
He knows what we are made of;
he remembers that we are dust.

PSALM 103:13-14 TEV

＊

I will lead the blind by ways they have not known,
along unfamiliar paths I will guide them;
I will turn the darkness into light before them
and make the rough places smooth.

ISAIAH 42:16

＊

[Jesus] said to her, "Daughter, your
faith has healed you. Go in peace."

LUKE 8:48

＊

If you have any encouragement from being united with Christ, if any comfort from his love, if any fellowship with the Spirit, if any tenderness and compassion, then make my joy complete by being like-minded, having the same love, being one in spirit and purpose.

Philippians 2:1-2

No one has ever seen God; but if we love one another, God lives in us and his love is made complete in us. We know that we live in him and he in us, because he has given us of his Spirit.

1 John 4:12-13

The Lamb at the center of the throne will be their shepherd; he will lead them to springs of living water. And God will wipe away every tear from their eyes.

Revelation 7:17

Remains to Be Seen

I've walked out of a bad movie before. I didn't care whether I saw the ending. But I'm a bit less casual when it comes to my life. I like to know how things will turn out. I like to see whether my efforts to help someone will pay off. I crave closure for past situations. I want distinct endings before I move on. And I long to know what my future holds.

Does it bug you when you only see a speck of the big picture? God calls you to pray, participate, follow, and surrender; he doesn't call you to do his job. When you move forward without seeing the whole picture, God is at work, making you whole.

With uncertainties circling about me and concerns facing my family, I'm not so good with letting go of the outcome. I pray for your will, and then I try to take back control. God, I want to rest in your embrace. I will trust you even when I'm scared.

Gusts of Grace

Trials sweep through your life like storm winds. They press you against a wall until you can't breathe. They bury you under burdens too heavy to lift on your own. Have you been thrown by such forces?

The trials that knock you off your feet are not strong enough or powerful enough to destroy the foundation of God's faithfulness. They're nothing compared to the gusts of grace that blow through us and clean out the loss, regret, and disappointment. Wait for his restoration. He will rebuild your life with the secure materials of grace and hope.

I'm still surprised I got out from under recent burdens. It was all your doing, Lord. I give you the credit and the praise. The struggle was so great, I couldn't move. You released me and gave me more strength and understanding to move forward into good things.

All Good

Unknowingly, we carry many wounds with us from the past into the present. We juggle shadows of them while trying to accomplish something new in our lives. We're so desperate to move on from trials that we neglect to glean the knowledge and understanding of God's faithfulness that comes from living our tough circumstances. So the pain stays with us.

Goodness can bloom from the hurtful experiences you've tried to forget. Those wounds helped shape who you are. Those wounds are part of the story of God's mercy. They're part of your journey from broken to whole.

I present a good front to others, but on the inside, a strong sense of failure burns. Help me to sit with the past rough parts of my journey. Help me to learn from them before I let them go. In your hands they become wisdom.

If It Ain't Broke

Most people would espouse the philosophy that it's best not to try to fix something that isn't blatantly broken. This seems like sage advice. We're busy, and we don't have time to waste. But because of this busyness, we often don't recognize when a part of us is broken and in dire need of fixing.

We juggle the needs of our families, we face obstacles with flair, and we keep life moving along. We bury our hurts and our needs under the demands of the day. The world might say to "leave well enough alone," but just getting by is not the same as wholeness. Life is intended to be abundant. Bring your brokenness to the Lord.

Time to be fixed. Time to admit I'm not perfect and that I'm not whole. I'm functional, and there's a big difference. Expose the broken places that I have skillfully patched up with human Band-Aid solutions. Grant me healing, God, from the inside out.

Between Engagements

Obligations. Responsibilities. Commitments. Events. Appointments. Has your personality taken on the characteristics of an overachiever, a chronic doer, a party planner? When activities shove aside active listening, praying, and meditating, you're usually left without energy, direction, or joy.

Give yourself room to think. Make time between engagements to engage in devotional living. If you rely on God to show up for everything you've penned into your week's schedule, isn't it time to show up for your Creator? No agenda in hand. No deadlines. Come to give and to be filled.

Lead me to the sanctuary of a quiet spirit. I haven't had that in a long time. I start out looking for peace but usually wind up volunteering for some task instead. I've depleted my reserves. Oh, how I long to be filled by your love, Lord.

Clank!

When I walk over to the long line of carts at the local wholesale store, I—without fail—select the cart with the loudest squeak and wobbliest wheel. Every time! It seems like too much effort to return it outside and select another... so I push on, pretending I don't hear the obnoxious, earsplitting clatter of my metal chariot.

We often maneuver through the tight turns of life with our broken parts and our human instability clanging away. All the while pretending we don't notice. All the while wishing we had exchanged our faults for forgiveness early on. Somehow we think it's noble to drag our loud problems with us rather than ask God to tend to them. We're so mistaken!

Oops. How loud are my problems? They certainly do clamor in my head and heart. God, give me the silence of well-being. Direct me toward measures of healing that soothe my spirit and seal my wounds for eternity.

Finding Yourself

The sculptor's hand can only break the spell,
To free the figures slumbering in the stone.

MICHELANGELO

When Michelangelo looked at a particular mass of stone, he saw his statue within. If we look at the mass of our ego, wants, needs, hurts, healings, faults, and strengths, can we see the "us" God created within? We must let God chip away those pieces that no longer belong in our lives (some never did belong). We must sculpt out our purpose with the chisel of faith and let our sins, heartaches, lies, and selfish desires tumble to the ground. Our way to wholeness begins with letting go.

I pray that I haven't disappointed you like I've disappointed myself. Lord, don't give up on me. Bless me with times of letting go so that the real me emerges complete and beautiful under the Creator's gaze.

Mine...Yours...God's

As a young girl, I read a story about two sisters who, after a fight, stretched a jump rope across the middle of their shared bedroom floor—each claimed sole occupancy of a half. Well, soon they both needed what was on the other's side, including the closet for clothes and the door to exit!

When we become judgmental, jealous, or self-righteous, we draw lines down the middle of our homes, churches, places of work, and neighborhoods. But we need others in order to live a whole life. Jesus tells us to "Love your neighbor" not because it's good PR for God, but because it's the way to wholeness, unity, and the expression of his heart.

Where are my dividing lines, God? I've lost track.
My envy or anger has established unnecessary
boundaries and limits in my life. Some relationships
have been repaired, but others remain in pieces.
Please heal my heart so that I will seek wholeness.

A Place to Belong

When visiting a small town, all it takes is one stop at the local market or the coffee shop and you're up on the news about colorful residents and the latest marriage and birth celebrations. In no time you can feel less of an outsider and more like a regular.

We all understand the desire to connect. God designed us to want to belong. For some it is less intense; for others it's motivation to create community wherever they go. Follow your heart when it is ready to connect with others. Step over the fear, insecurity, or obstacles, and trust the longing that leads to wholeness through fellowship.

God, I feel the tug to join in and to be a part of life around me, yet I use my family's needs and schedule as an excuse to keep a distance. Lead me to the right people. I want to belong and feel the wholeness of community.

A Whole Life

During each life season we tend to define our existence by a few things: School and work. Work and dating. Work and marriage. Marriage and family. Children and parents. What defines your life right now? Consider expanding the list. Our priorities will take up more of our time and effort, but they should not replace a complete life.

Open up to your spiritual growth, friendships, development of your gifts, service to those outside of your family, commitment to follow through in areas you've short-changed. Talk to God about what your life needs in order to be whole again.

I haven't felt complete in a while. My life seems to be all about family. It's good, yet I feel an ache for friendships and a hunger for faith. God, help me to find a balance so that I can serve my priorities and seek a whole, fulfilling life that pleases you.

Discovery

Words of Discovery

Can you discover the limits and bounds of
the greatness and power of God? The sky
is no limit for God, but it lies beyond your
reach. God knows the world of the dead,
but you do not know it. God's greatness is
broader than the earth, wider than the sea.

JOB 11:7-9 TEV

O God, you are my God, earnestly I seek you;
my soul thirsts for you, my body longs for you,
in a dry and weary land where there is no water.

PSALM 63:1

Beg for knowledge; plead for insight.
Look for it as hard as you would for silver
or some hidden treasure. If you do, you will know
what it means to fear the LORD
and you will succeed in learning about God.
It is the LORD who gives wisdom;
from him come knowledge and understanding.

PROVERBS 2:3-6 TEV

Do not abandon wisdom, and she will protect you; love her, and she will keep you safe. Getting wisdom is the most important thing you can do. Whatever else you get, get insight. Love wisdom, and she will make you great. Embrace her, and she will bring you honor. She will be your crowning glory.

PROVERBS 4:6-9 TEV

From now on I will tell you of new things, of hidden things unknown to you.

ISAIAH 48:6

You will call upon me and come and pray to me, and I will listen to you. You will seek me and find me when you seek me with all your heart.

JEREMIAH 29:12-13

Without faith it is impossible to please God, because anyone who comes to him must believe that he exists and that he rewards those who earnestly seek him.

HEBREWS 11:6

Turning Corners

I love to walk through a city for hours. Unlike suburbs where one uninterrupted main road can run the length of a development or a community, the city offers the gift of blocks. I walk so many strides, and there I am, standing at a new corner. I can turn the corner and encounter a new discovery, adventure, and view.

In your life you'll encounter long, continuous parts of your path. But just when you have the horizon memorized, an intersection in the form of a decision, a revelation, or a change will present itself. God is leading you to turn a new corner in your life! Embrace the discoveries up ahead.

I'm a bit nervous but also excited. I know change is coming, and I welcome it. Only when I embrace the opportunities to rely on you completely will I ever discover the lessons and wonders you want me to gather.

Enjoy the Unexpected

A sense of control is important in a woman's life. People are depending on us! Managing time, family details, and finances is a good thing. But don't let the necessity of organization turn into a need to control everything that comes along—people, conversations, and opportunities.

My quest to control the unexpected has brought with it more sorrow than satisfaction. Can you relate? It can feel so right to take charge, but by doing so, we cut short the blessings God presents. And we miss out on the unexpected delights that come our way!

Tightness in the pit of my stomach is my usual warning that I'm about to lose control of a situation. God, why am I so anxious? I have great faith in you. It would be so nice to enjoy the gifts of unexpected events, people, and possibilities. Free me from myself, Lord.

Leading Lady

In the movie *The Holiday* there's a scene where a main character is lamenting her heartbreak…caused by a louse. The older gentleman dining with her is a retired screenwriter from Hollywood's glamour days; he sums up her problem: she always casts herself as the "friend" when she is meant to be the leading lady!

Become the leading lady of your life. This doesn't mean you upstage others at work. It doesn't mean you are never a friend. It does mean that you stop trying to be someone you aren't, and you step up into the role God has shaped for you. Brilliant.

God, show me what it takes to be the leading lady of my life. I can't wait to walk with confidence, knowing that I'm not pretending but am purposed for this path and part. Give me the courage to step forward as I trust your direction.

Harvest of Honor

You reap what you sow. Don't let the common usage of this faith formula deceive you. It has great significance for your daily life and your future. Are you harvesting good behaviors, relationships, and experiences in each season of your life? If not, what is in your sower's pouch?

If you regularly reap half-truths or unfulfilled promises, examine whether you are planting honesty and faithfulness. Are you up front with yourself, God, and others? Do you follow through? Ask God for the seeds of wisdom, sincerity, and integrity, and offer him a heart prepared to grow goodness.

I want to invest my efforts in goodness. Give
me the right seeds to plant at the right time.
I will nurture them and lift their harvest
up to you. I hope to reap good relationships,
kindness, faithfulness, and joy to honor you.

Creation in Motion

You're part of the history of the world and the history of God's people. When you think of your life as insignificant—a blip on the eternity screen—you're forgetting how vital your role is. Each story of faith is remarkable. Each life lived under God's grace is a testimony. Each woman's journey as a person of prayer and purpose is monumental.

God sees you. Your heart, your faults, your gifts, your truth. You are a part of creation in motion. Those who came before and those who come after will never offer God or the world the gift of you. Give it and live it! Start to see what God sees in you!

My days matter. My prayers matter. My commitment to faith matters. Show me how to communicate my testimony. I don't feel like I have enough to say, but I know you give every person the power of a story. May my dependence on you be the theme of mine.

Look for It!

Along the shore there are many discoveries to be made. Some rest on the sand's surface, just waiting to be plucked and carried away by a lucky person. Other ocean prizes lie under the rough surface. They won't be found by the lucky, but by the diligent.

Do you gather those treasures that sit atop the path but never look more carefully for those blessings below the surface of conversation, daily living, and brief encounters? Head out into your life with watchful eyes and an attentive heart, and don't forget your yellow plastic shovel. Go deeper. Be the one to discover the buried gems.

God, give me patience to persevere in my search for life's treasures. I'll watch more carefully. I'll stop and pay attention. I'll keep digging until you tell me to stop.

Connecting

My interactions with others can be filled with small talk or distracted conversation. These half-hearted connections with coworkers, family, friends, and strangers aren't because I don't care; they happen because my head is in the clouds or my heart is buried under the weight of worry—either way, I'm bypassing the significance of relationships.

Honor the value of the people God brings to your path. Focus on what they say with their words and with their silence. When responsibilities and commitments fill your mind, your choice to be present for people will lead you to be present in your life.

I want my connections with others to be sincere.
God, when I start to check out of conversations
or my responsibilities to others, lead me back
to focus. May I honor you by honoring others
and savoring the present moment.

Under the Sun

The author of Ecclesiastes hungered to find the meaning of life. But as he examined wealth, labor, freedom, and decadence, he discovered that life itself was meaningless. "What has been will be again, what has been done will be done again; there is nothing new under the sun" (Ecclesiastes 1:9). How can this fit with the faith journey?

Ecclesiastes illuminates the most important truth you can discover: There's nothing of the world you can pursue that will give your life purpose and significance. Not money. Not success. Not a house. Not a picket fence. Not celebrity. Only the pursuit of God will give your life meaning. Following the way of God is the only journey that matters.

I've felt the emptiness of shallow pursuits and the sadness of meaningless endeavors. Only when I came to your heart did I discover purpose for the rest of my journey. There's nothing under the sun more meaningful than the Maker of the sun and his love.

Belief

Words for Belief

I trust in your unfailing love;
my heart rejoices in your salvation.

PSALM 13:5

Trust in the LORD and do good;
dwell in the land and enjoy safe pasture.
Delight yourself in the LORD
and he will give you the
desires of your heart.

PSALM 37:3-4

Commit your way to the LORD;
trust in him and he will do this:
He will make your righteousness
shine like the dawn,
the justice of your cause
like the noonday sun.

PSALM 37:5-6

Blessed is the man who makes
the LORD his trust,
who does not look to the proud,
to those who turn aside to false gods.

PSALM 40:4

⸺

When I am afraid, I will trust in you.
In God, whose word I praise,
in God I trust; I will not be afraid.
What can mortal man do to me?

PSALM 56:3-4

⸺

Look, you are trusting in deceptive
words that are worthless.

JEREMIAH 7:8

⸺

In him and through faith in
him we may approach God with
freedom and confidence.

EPHESIANS 3:12

⸺

Reaching for Faith

When I stand my ground and insist that belief has not worked, that faith has let me down, it is usually after I have taken a tumble. Wouldn't faith in God—wouldn't God for that matter—make sure that I didn't end up here again…in the mess of mistake and regret.

But even the huge blind spot of my denial is not big enough, or permanent enough, for me to eventually see that it was my doing that led to my undoing. Sometimes I can even see the life rafts, wake-up calls, or yield signs God provided. Don't let belief become your scapegoat. If you believe, walk in it. And when you fall, cling to it.

I'm sitting here in the middle of my latest mistake. I want to blame you for my frailty when actually it is my fragile state of life that gives me the greatest insight into your presence. Lead me toward belief in my purpose so that I can let go of excuses and reach for faith.

Fearless

Do you worry a lot about your safety? Are you afraid of what people think of you? Do you read about the possible side effects of your medications and then become convinced that you feel every one? It is normal for active minds to go the way of "what if something bad happens," but before these thoughts gain too much influence, it is vital to turn them over to God. Replace the fear of harm with faith in him.

Placing your trust in God completely will change your life and your thinking. Even everyday concerns will be cast in a new light. Nothing can hurt the heart that is held in God's hands.

I trust you. I trust in you. I entrust my life to you. I give you my thoughts, actions, worries, and preoccupation with image. Things do and can go wrong. Help me not beckon them with added worry, but actually release them from my thoughts. Fill my mind with your promises.

Spiritual Development

Building up our belief system can require that we build up immunities on a spiritual level. As we are exposed to tests of faith, to trials, and to rocky days, we are developing stronger spiritual responses. We learn when we take our comfort in God, and we gain knowledge when we seek guidance in his Word.

If we respond to situations out of an absolute trust in God, eventually our attitudes and belief will follow. Our reliance on God becomes second nature as we relinquish our human nature and take on a new identity in Christ.

I'm facing a new day with new possibilities. God, help me react to each situation, person, decision, and opportunity with complete faith. I want to walk in goodness and righteousness. May the longings of my heart begin to take on the shape of your will for my life. Give me clarity so that my first response comes from a pure desire to please you.

Faith Thesaurus

My family watches a popular game show because it is all about words. It is fun to fill in some of the missing letters and guess the word or phrase that is up on the screen with a few gaping holes in it. It also challenges one's mind to think through more words and to learn new ones along the way.

Are you spending time searching for words that fill you and feed you? The other words—ones that belittle, reject, and negate life and God's children—are all around you. So all the more reason to expand your personal thesaurus of positivisms; you can share goodness, peace, hope, encouragement, acceptance, and belief every time it's your turn!

Clean up my language, Lord. I use so many negative expressions and share so much of my inner turmoil, that I bypass all the joy and the good things I know. I want to pass along the words of strength, power, love, and forgiveness you give to me. You are the Word—may I express you every day.

Radiant Faith

We replaced our heater with a blower because it was loud, used up a lot of energy, and was either on or off, rather than constantly emanating warmth. Now we have a radiant heater placed in the corner of our living room that warms our old house during winter.

The way we share our faith can be a lot like these forms of heat. Some people are "on" all the time and loud about their faith. This kind of witness can be powerful, but it can also feel forced rather than authentic. When you are strong in your belief, you can stand quietly among others and still radiate the warmth of faith—peace, love, kindness, truth.

Help me radiate with your love. When I force my beliefs and become loud about my righteousness, it is usually all about me, and not about you. I want my life to emit the serenity, mercy, and warmth I receive unconditionally from you.

Even in the Unknowing

When television shows, news segments, or Internet highlights present the hard and sad things going on near or far, our feelings of distress can be so overwhelming that we forget to rest in God. We can turn our anxiety over to God in prayer. He's already on it, you can be sure. And the more we give our fears up to God's care, the better able we are to embrace peace and hope and act on our compassion and empathy.

How we face the unknowns can build up or dismantle the foundation of faith. We can't be sure what tomorrow will bring to us and to others in the world, but we can find our solid footing in the known, in the absolutes of God's faithfulness.

God, I want to feel for those in pain. I want to rise up and speak for those who face injustice. I want to be strong for those who are fragile. To do these things, I must first trust you. May I stop trembling in my insecurities here on the bridge of fear and cross to the safe refuge of your understanding. You don't ask me to know all or be prepared for every possible happening; you ask only that I believe, and that I move forward in that belief.

Staying Focused

Who, what, where, when, how? Our minds sift through these questions constantly. We are always on a quest for answers. Big or small, these questions often end up directing our lives. But shouldn't the answers be what guide our steps? How long do you wait for word from God before you start asking more questions or create an answer of your own?

As we continue to ask questions, we will learn and grow. But we will be blessed when we pause long enough to listen for what God is saying.

I so want to know the future and my purpose and the outcome to decisions I made a week ago, last year...God, help me stay focused on the priorities you give me right now. Grant me the patience and the courage to move forward even when question marks fill my thoughts. It is enough that I know the One who holds all the answers.

Heartbreak Belief

Has love ever come at a price in your life? What has been your experience? Love certainly requires sacrifice; that is to be expected. What we don't anticipate are the times when love breaks us or breaks our trust. It is difficult to consider loving again until healing comes.

God heals us with saving grace. Divine faithfulness mends torn trusts; our identity becomes tied to wholeness rather than wrapped up in broken dreams. Your spiritual heart is not lost, nor is it dangling by a man-made, fragile thread. It is intact and connected to God's heart. Love does come at a price, but the price has been paid.

You've been with me through my heartache. There were times I could barely breathe. I know that you carried me. Even now, you are still carrying me through and over the remains of past pain. Thank you for never losing sight of me. I felt so small, insignificant, and lost. You held me in your hand so that I would feel the strength and power of true love.

How Do I Look?

If we do an abdominal workout every day for one month, we kinda hope someone notices. If we have our hair cut in a new style, we want to look fresh. Yet when we spend time in devotions, prayer, and fellowship, are we expecting results? Are we anticipating that a noticeable change will occur? We should.

When we nurture our spiritual lives, there will be an outward manifestation of a renewed, stronger faith. "The fruit of the Spirit is love, joy, peace, patience, kindness, goodness, faithfulness, gentleness and self-control" (Galatians 5:22-23). The results of spiritual growth go beyond our hearts and souls and become visible as the harvest is lived out.

*God, help me remember that a renewed
mind and heart should be visible as I practice
patience and self-control, express kindness,
turn toward love and joy, speak for peace, act
out of faithfulness, and offer gentleness.*

Miracle of Belief

To expand my faith, I decided to pay attention to all the miracles around me and to determine which was the greatest. I noted the countless little blooms on each lilac, the shadows cast by the sun, the intricacy of the human eye, a friend's comment that brought me awareness and comfort. The list was endless as soon as it began.

With God's fingerprints everywhere I looked, it occurred to me what the greatest miracle was—out of thin air, completely real, and the one thing that tied me to all the miracles—my belief.

Thank you for my belief. Through years of questions and private doubts, I feel the depth of the miracle of faith. It gives me new life, new eyes for your work, and a heart that knows its Maker.

Perseverance

Words for Perseverance

Love the LORD your God with all
your heart and with all your soul
and with all your strength.

DEUTERONOMY 6:5

The fear of the LORD is the
beginning of wisdom;
all who follow his precepts have
good understanding.
To him belongs eternal praise.

PSALM 111:10

Great is our Lord and mighty in power;
his understanding has no limit.
The LORD sustains the humble
but casts the wicked to the ground.

PSALM 147:5-6

The LORD is my strength and my shield;
my heart trusts in him, and I am helped.

PSALM 28:7

⁓

The LORD gives strength to his people;
the LORD blesses his people with peace.

PSALM 29:11

⁓

When Pilate heard this, he was even
more afraid, and he went back inside the
palace. "Where do you come from?" he
asked Jesus, but Jesus gave him no answer.
"Do you refuse to speak to me?" Pilate
said. "Don't you realize I have power
either to free you or to crucify you?"

JOHN 19:8-10

⁓

What Now?

Have you reached your "what now" point? It's pretty easy to recognize; in fact, you may have been here before. It happens when your cleverness and education and Internet-search savvy stop being enough to get by. You've tapped all your resources to solve a problem, create a different outcome, or make a change.

"What now" can be a very fruitful time of awakening. Use it to embrace your limits rather than resist them, and turn to God's strength for whatever is next.

Okay, God, I am here. I've tried everything, and I know I can't fix my life or even my current situation. I should've learned this lesson years ago, but I resisted it. I want to trust in your strength. I want to face whatever is next and know that you're in control.

All We Need

The more you know about God, the more you know you need God. A desire to be faithful, righteous, and godly leads us to the Cross. When difficulties rise up, our hearts know where home is. We long for communion with God and the comfort of his leading. We seek his wisdom and truths so that our lives are based on solid ground.

We tend to look at a need as something that is missing, when really our needs are our stepping stones back to God's love and guidance. Our lack is his abundance. Our doubt is his assurance. And our weakness is his strength.

Take me to your heart, God. I want to just be in your presence so that I can know you better. My wants tend to lead me back to myself. My needs direct me back to you, my Creator. Only you truly know what I need to carry on.

Leapin' Faith

Kids like to take flying leaps from edges of pools, jungle gyms, or stairs and holler "Catch me." Sometimes their request is said too late, or their weight and enthusiasm creates an uncatchable human cannonball. Not good.

There is a fruitful time and place for us to throw ourselves on God's strength. I suppose anytime is still considered a leap of faith, but when we do it in the midst of dire straits or midjump after *we've* made a big decision without his earlier input, we are really testing the limits of reality more than we are giving ourselves over to God's strength and purpose. Are you at a place of decision? Try praying "Catch me" *before* you are midflight.

I'm so close to leaping. I think on things for so very long that I begin to lose my nerve. Now I can barely hold myself back. God, please give me the patience to wait on your guidance and direction. Give me peace and leading before I jump into a decision made by me on my terms.

The Great Exchange

It only takes me a couple of visits to the gym to realize how limited my physical strength is. And it only takes me a couple of exposures to trials to realize how limited my spiritual and emotional strength is. Thank goodness that we are supposed to hand over our measly human power and exchange it for God's might.

We might want to use God like an on-call personal trainer or life coach, but when we do, we are still holding on to our limited version of life. Give over what you've got, and take on the amazing, boundless power of God.

I'm handing over my very limited strength, God. I've given things my best effort and have realized that you want something even more for me than the results I've managed. I only see what is humanly possible; you see what is ultimately possible.

Reaching Higher

I know it is easy to think you can do it all on your own. Sometimes that is exactly how we get as far as we do—because we are independent and have had to stand alone for whatever reason. This personal gusto and ambition can light a fire under the human spirit, but the good news about your life of faith is that it is ignited by the Holy Spirit.

Faith isn't asking for a handout or even a hand up; it is acknowledging that you are not standing alone, but on the shoulders of God.

Faith has helped me get to where I am. But my lack of faith has kept me from reaching beyond my abilities. I'm desperately in need of your shoulders to stand on. It is tough to lose my footing on the earth, but I want my reach to be that much closer to the sky.

Let Your Heart Lead

When I get really stressed, my thoughts become scattered. I'm forgetful. My words get jumbled, I can't listen to what others are saying, and my logic is less than solid. When I do speak a full sentence, I can be insensitive without knowing it. Have you been there?

When your mind is preoccupied or taken over by stressbrain, it is more important than ever to spend time in prayer. Becoming centered on God and his presence will still the emotions, the spinning thoughts, and the panic. So don't worry. The next time your mind is juggling life's details badly, go to your heart for answers.

God, I'm spending time here in my heart with you. I like the peace, the inspiration, and the comfort that fills me. So often I come to you with just my thoughts, my data from the day; may I learn to start from my heart so that I am capable of hearing you clearly.

Beyond Our Limits

After many years of dependence on glasses, I couldn't wait to have lasik eye surgery. Immediately after, I could see the clock on the wall. Within days I drove to the coast. But months later when I couldn't see the writing on a sign aisles away at a store, I was disappointed—my miracle had blurry edges—until a friend with glasses said she couldn't even see the sign.

As with our vision, our human perspective will always have limits. God's clarity is forever. There are no cloudy moments. God knows truth beyond our deepest questions. God sees beyond our blurry, short-sighted goals. God's understanding has no limit.

You see all, know all, and understand all. My vision is so limited. As I push on toward my immediate goals and my next destination, I cannot see up ahead. I must trust you and entrust to you my entire journey.

Let Go My Ego

Have you ever faced a challenge head-on and left God out of it? Do you sometimes let doubt lead you back to self-reliance? It is human to have questions and even to question God. But when you offer up your strength and ability as the solution rather than trust God, you will keep running into yourself and the same ol' problems you always bring to the table.

The strength of the Almighty is working through you. Don't miss out on it!

Lord, stop me from interfering so much. I want to take over every situation. Figuring out faith is hard. Forgive me when I take a shortcut by trying to do it my way. I promise to come to you with my doubts and concerns. When my ego tries to take your place, remind me how that tends to get me in trouble!

In the Will

What would you do or say or overcome in order to be first in line for a large family inheritance? This might be a theme for numerous Hollywood films, but it isn't presented to many of us in real life. Too bad. Or is it?

Real security isn't about getting in the good graces of a wealthy distant relative. Thank goodness we have a wealthy, close God. His abundance is given freely to all his children. Struggles will come, but they will be used toward growing a deeper faith and a greater understanding of grace. When we place our hope in God's strength, our future security is immediate.

I love that as I seek and walk in your will, I am in your eternal will—I have an inheritance that surpasses earthly dollars. There is so much more security and peace of mind and spirit that comes with the legacy of your grace and compassion.

Waiting Rooms

I've had my share of hospital waiting rooms lately. I'm not a fan. Thankfully some hospitals now have pagers, similar to those handed out at restaurants on a Saturday night, with flashing lights to announce your spot in the medical lineup. I like them because they are a pass to step beyond the sliding doors and into the sun where I can breathe.

Our faith is a pass to more hopeful times of waiting. We still go through the experience, but it is less about enduring and more about nurturing and understanding. Let God show you a new way to persevere. The light we hold from him gives freedom and rest.

You know I hate to wait. I was about to implode
when a new perspective of faith came to me. I finally
understood that when I'm waiting, I'm not restricted
to a sterile, unnourished life. You still cover me,
you carry me, and you calm my impatient spirit.

Joy

Words for Joy

The LORD your God will bless you in all
your harvest and in all the work of your
hands, and your joy will be complete.

DEUTERONOMY 16:15

Nehemiah said, "Go and enjoy choice
food and sweet drinks, and send some to
those who have nothing prepared. This
day is sacred to our Lord. Do not grieve,
for the joy of the LORD is your strength."

NEHEMIAH 8:10

You make me glad by your deeds, O LORD;
I sing for joy at the works of your hands.

PSALM 92:4

Those who sow in tears
will reap with songs of joy.

PSALM 126:5

A man finds joy in giving an apt reply—
and how good is a timely word!

PROVERBS 15:23

I have told you this so that my joy may be in
you and that your joy may be complete.

JOHN 15:11

Out of the most severe trial, their
overflowing joy and their extreme
poverty welled up in rich generosity.

2 CORINTHIANS 8:2

In all my prayers for all of you,
I always pray with joy.

PHILIPPIANS 1:4

Good Times

It is healing to laugh. A good movie, a great conversation, or a comic moment can lift my spirits. I feel physically lighter and more hopeful when laughter has been a part of my day. I can be facing big challenges, and yet the mere recollection of a funny incident can shift everything toward hope.

Joy can give us that ongoing path toward hope. It isn't dependent upon humor but is inspired by faith and contentment. It is a brightness that does not fade.

Thank you for the gift of laughter. When it comes along, I am reminded of the simplicity of pure happiness. Show me how I can go beyond occasional moments of lightness to an ongoing, ever-flowing sense of joy and peace.

Generate Joy

Do you light up a room when you walk in? Okay, do you make others feel accepted and appreciated? Does your attitude express your faith, or does it keep others at a distance? As people of faith, we don't always have to be "on," and we don't have to present a perfect life. But we will live a more meaningful life if we generate joy around us through genuine kindness and interest in the well-being of others.

Your light can be a simple greeting, an offer of help, a warm welcome.

God, nudge me when I have a chance to extend friendship to another. Open my eyes to the times when others are reaching out to me. I want to see each person just as you do. Help me sense their heart needs so that I can respond with kindness and thoughtfulness.

What You Make It

I have a lot of deadlines. I need to get to the dentist. The vet keeps sending me postcards for my cats' annual shots. My car needs an oil change. And I haven't gone grocery shopping in two weeks. Some days when I'm scrambling to stay afloat, I have to ask "Shouldn't there be more to my life experience?"

There it is. Like a life raft floating within reach—joy. Buoyant. Available. Just waiting for me to grab hold of it. As responsibilities rise and fall like waves around me, I am able to stay afloat. I feel lighter. And the view from this particular day, this moment, is sacred.

Forgive me for focusing so much on the work of living that I forget to celebrate the wonder and joy. You have made the life experience complex and overflowing with goodness. Help me grab hold of the mystery and the delight of being alive.

Grief Encounter

Sorrow can seep into the body, the mind, and the spirit. It can settle in between our bones and thoughts and drift into our dreams. When our journey takes us through grief, our cries rise up beyond our physical life and become prayers for peace. God hears us and leads our hearts toward the possibility of transformation.

As we turn over our sorrow to God's care, our weeping turns to song. Our mourning turns to joy. Our brokenness turns to wholeness. Our poverty of spirit turns to wealth of hope.

God, I can't see beyond the hurt right now. I'm entrusting the pain and the loss to your hands. It is a relief to know that even when I don't know what to say, you hear my cries, and you prepare a way for me to find peace once again.

Praise

God amazes me. He baffles me too, but mostly he surprises me with the incredible moments of happiness that come my way. I want to praise God when the wave of joy floods my being. Like a parent beaming at the sight of her baby's smile, God must also connect to his children's pleasure with equal joy.

When delight brightens your countenance, turn your face upward in gratitude—your heart will follow, and you will see a reflection of God's gladness.

With all the joys I savor in life, may I remember to lift up my gladness to you in praise. Those moments of deep delight are a gift. Help me to acknowledge them and to hold them close so that the echoes of each joy stay with me through the days of my life.

After Party

Trials will befall our paths and the paths of those we love most. What I'm discovering is that after the trials there does come a time of relief and joy. When you aren't expecting it, flashes of happiness surface after a long absence.

You might not even know how to respond to joy because it is in such contrast to the hardship. But God does lead you out of the desert of loss or trouble. He invites your spirit to reawaken to joy so that you can celebrate the blessing of his love through the journey and on the other side of this hardship.

*I'm not ready for balloons and party invitations. I ache
inside, and I have days that seem covered in clouds.
But I'm beginning to feel again—the hurt is there,
but it has made room for moments of peace, and they
are so refreshing. Thank you for remembering me,
God. Thank you for restoring my capacity for joy.*

Thinking of You

Who brings a smile to your face? Who was the one who gave you confidence to reach for your dreams? Who offered you help and empathy when you felt so alone? Consider the many friends and strangers God has brought to your experience. It does the spirit good to think about the times you felt deep connection to God through another human being.

Take time to reflect fondly on those people who have touched your life. It does the heart wonders to realize that your joy is their joy, their happiness is your happiness. This is community, this is fellowship, this is God.

How have I forgotten the lovely people you have brought me closer to in one way or another? It is such a gift to think of past friends or mentors or even role models I've never met. God, today I lift up those people and pray joy for their lives.

Let Loose

Something changes in my spirit when a laugh or a smile emerges seemingly out of nowhere. Suddenly all the adult pressures are gone. I used to squelch the strong impulses of joy, because they can come over me when I should be focused, or serious, or worried, or in charge. I'm learning to loosen up and embrace each time joy shines on my life.

As a child, did you laugh a lot with a certain friend, or find great happiness when a teacher helped you tap in to a passion for learning, or stare with fascination at a ladybug resting on your flip-flop in the summer sun? Don't restrict your happiness...recapture the pure joy of living!

Why don't I let myself enjoy life more? Since when does growing up mean giving up abundant, pleasurable living? No more! I promise to indulge in laughter and contentment, God. The delights of being your child are too great to count, so I will gather what I can and say thank you!

Rearview-Mirror Lessons

When I think back over my life, there were times when worries about my work, an important decision, or the future occupied my every thought. Each concern seemed like it was the biggest and most pivotal fork in the road I would ever face. Now I understand that God does carry us through these worries.

What seems insurmountable today may very well be tomorrow's testimony of joy. Hindsight is a great teacher. Each stumbling block becomes another opportunity to trust God. Let today's burden transform to blessing as you give it over to God's care.

I've gotta say, I'm ready for this current burden
to become a lesson learned, a story of faith, a past
trial I lean upon for new strength. But as much
as I want it to be over, God, I know that you
are calling me to be very present, aware, awake,
and faithful while this hardship unfolds.

Joy Full

What fills you? What interests, gifts, talents, passions, and dreams inspire you? There are so many activities and details that deplete our energy and happiness reserves, making it vital to understand what things or people or pursuits fill us back up.

God's love is an endless source of hope and contentment. Once you begin to trust that he is always there for you and that he made you unique and wonderful...you can turn each day into a chance to discover more about yourself, the God who loves you, and what fills you with deep joy.

I want to immerse myself in the joy that comes from you, God. I want to be surrounded by it, filled with it, and eager to share it with others. Discovering more about my unique self and purpose in you replenishes my spirit, my hope, and my faith.

Character

Words for Character

I know, my God, that you test the
heart and are pleased with integrity.
All these things have I given
willingly and with honest intent.

1 CHRONICLES 29:17

My soul clings to you;
your right hand upholds me.

PSALM 63:8

The LORD will keep you from all harm—
he will watch over your life;
the LORD will watch over
your coming and going
both now and forevermore.

PSALM 121:7-8

Then you will understand
what is right and just
and fair—every good path.
For wisdom will enter your heart,
and knowledge will be
pleasant to your soul.

PROVERBS 2:9-10

Where, then, is boasting? It is excluded.
On what principle? On that of observing
the law? No, but on that of faith. For
we maintain that a man is justified by
faith apart from observing the law.

ROMANS 3:27-28

Each man should give what he has decided
in his heart to give, not reluctantly or under
compulsion, for God loves a cheerful giver.

2 CORINTHIANS 9:7

Keeping It Equal

I want to believe that if I have more wealth, more security, and more of the world's foundation beneath my feet...I will be a better person. I'll serve God enthusiastically. My thoughts will quickly turn to the needy. I'll be generous in heart and spirit. Yet, I know that having more does not lead to more generosity, integrity, and service.

With more money comes more responsibility, obligation, and pressure. That's the formula of the world. God's formula for a good life is to give more than we have. To give freely of our heart, our service, our devotion, and our compassion no matter our earnings. In fact, your net worth is totally unrelated to your actual worth. Let that truth shape your character and how you spend your heart.

Can I help it if I want the security of the world? It is hard to let go of that. It is all that I see around me. Your ways can feel distant, God. Direct my eyes to all that you are and all that I am supposed to become. Let these define me. Lead me not to security but to generosity of heart and blessing.

You Tell Me

I wait and I wait for an answer sometimes. I pray for it. I watch for it. I ask others to pray for it and watch for it. I tap my toes. I count the ceiling tiles. I watch seasons come and go. I know there are lessons during this seeming interlude. Who am I when I'm not given what I demand right away? Who am I when I'm dependent on God completely?

It would be nice if we always had certainty about God's will and next step for us. But then we wouldn't have the wisdom that does come during the waiting and the watching. We are being shaped with great precision during those times. Don't miss it.

I am waiting, Lord. You are probably waiting as well...for me to grow a little, rest a little, settle into contentment for once in my life, and to trust you completely. Waiting used to seem like a waste; now I know that it was my misuse of the waiting that has been wasteful. Forgive me, and help me trust.

Deal or No Deal

What temptations cause you to undermine your values, your measures of decency? Are you solid in a sense of self and faith until you face off with a particular roadblock? Sex, gambling, money, anger, impatience, greed, insecurity, competition, judgment? It feels good to rule out a few of these with a clear "Oh, I never struggle with *that!*" But there are probably a few on this list or in your life that are a constant struggle.

Think through the sins, the temptations that put your sanity and purpose at risk. We all have points of weakness, but what we do with them determines our spiritual health and recovery. Give them each, one by one, over to God in prayer regularly. Confronting such problems means you are regaining strength over them, by the grace of God.

That bad habit of mine…the rationalizing…it has to go. God help me when I start making deals with my integrity, my dreams, my beliefs. When I look at my life and my troubles, I see a list of reoccurring struggles. May I relinquish control of all these areas to your world-creating, future-shaping power!

Caving In (It Can Be Good)

Have you ever strongly felt the urge to do something because it was right or loving or necessary…and yet you wanted to fight it off? I have. I worry if I give myself over to the still small voice of God, I'll lose my own voice. I worry that this one step will turn into one hundred more, and I just don't have that kind of energy.

When we feel that urge toward goodness, wholeness, service, hospitality, or kindness, none of the worries matter. Really. Take the plunge. Cave in to conscience, give in to God's leading, and dive in to divine intervention. This is not only freeing, it is the beginning of all-out faithful living.

Break down the barriers to my heart. Lead me to let go of my hang-ups so that I can reach out to others when the time is right. When I try to let myself off the hook because I am busy or uncertain, remind me that my life is bigger than I am. Remind me that you have plans beyond my own.

It's the Little Things

The other day I made a really good choice. I knew I wouldn't see the end result. And I had to sacrifice something I cared about. I know, it isn't about me; but the truth is that I was elated. All day I felt good about the chance to make something right in the world. It was God who made it happen, but I was a part of it. I asked God to use me and he did.

We have many opportunities to serve this world and the God who made it. Don't wait for grand gestures. Stop where you are right now. Grab on to the opportunity in front of you.

Open my eyes to the little things today. Reveal to me the ways that my attitude and my behavior and my choices can serve you and your children.

Great Intentions

I mean to do well. Don't we all? We wake up, set out for the day, and have every intention of making it through with a bit of integrity and grace. Do you stumble as much as I do? Do you not even notice until the mishap has happened, the hurtful action has injured another, or the misstep trampled all over someone's feelings?

Often our first response is really our very human response that is shaped by fatigue, anger, envy, or shortsightedness. Turn good intentions into God's intended wisdom for your steps, decisions, and responses.

*God, protect others from my times of weakness when
I say words that can hurt their feelings. Help me
hold my tongue before I unleash my problems, my
issues, my fears on some undeserving soul! Lord,
I want to keep my intentions pure and right.*

Needy and in Need

To be deemed clingy in our society is to be considered a failure, a person who requires the endless support, energy, and pity of others. But in spiritual terms, clinging to God and his power is a sign of strength. It does the soul well to reach out to God in total dependence. Only then are we drawing our identity from the one true power.

The undesirable form of neediness is born of many unmet, buried, real needs; don't hold back from connecting to God or to those he gives you who can offer friendship, support, and guidance. You are made to need God's mercy and wisdom.

I resist being dependent upon you, God. I've tried to go it alone for a long time. But life is giving me cause to reevaluate this stance. I need you. There it is. I need you and your strength and your salvation and your mercy.

Glad Someone Notices

There is much I like to hide about my life. I don't tell others about my eating habits, the thoughts I harbor, the moments when anger consumes me, or the way I space off when I should be working. But as ashamed as I am of these and other indiscretions, there is a part of me that is very thankful that God sees my comings and my goings; he witnesses my heart in its goodness and stubbornness. And he still loves me.

There is freedom in having accountability to your Maker. There is such sweetness in God's grace, but first we must surrender the good, the bad, the semicrazy, and the mistakes. At the end of the day you will be glad that someone noticed you...all of you.

The shelter of your love protects me. You know all and see all. I am continuously amazed that you do not reject me for my past mistakes and current fumblings. You teach me and lead me, and you care about the person I become. Thank you for seeing all of me.

Big Head

Do we really think we understand the mechanics of life, biology, spirituality, purpose, or relationship better than the One who made them? I confess some days I actually *do*. Conceit inflates my false sense of security like a rubber raft setting sail for the New World (where I am the leader, of course). And like most overused inflatable items, my ego is destined for a leak, a pop, or a slow fizzle into nothing more than apologies and humiliation.

God desires to see us through to purpose, fulfillment, and knowledge. We just have to learn to seek godly actions instead of I-am-God delusions.

Yep. I do think I know best a lot of times, even though my track record would prove otherwise. I'm stubborn, God. I believe in you, but I let my agenda and ego take over. Let my recent mistakes be gentle reminders of how fallible my judgment can be and how enormous my need for you is.

What Is Left?

After hardship comes and goes, after moods swing us from here to there, after sugar highs turn to lows, we are left with ourselves—the tears, fears, successes, joys, and dreams. And there's more. Beyond these we can discover even more about ourselves. When we look at our identity as a child of God, our true core is witnessed.

See the you God is proud of. See the you God leads through a life patterned after no other. When emotions and aspirations fade, the truth of who you are in God radiates.

I've had my share of highs and lows. I realize how my mood and my sense of value impacts my response to circumstances when I should be turning to my faith response. Guide me to rely on your love and instruction as my foundation for all that I do and all that I am.

Security

Words for Security

Not one of all the LORD's good
promises to the house of Israel
failed; every one was fulfilled.

JOSHUA 21:45

I will establish my covenant with you, and
you will know that I am the LORD.

EZEKIEL 16:62

I say to you: Ask and it will be given to you;
seek and you will find; knock and the door
will be opened to you. For everyone who
asks receives; he who seeks finds; and to
him who knocks, the door will be opened.

LUKE 11:9-10

I will do whatever you ask in my name, so
that the Son may bring glory to the Father.

JOHN 14:13

This is the covenant I will make with them
after that time, says the Lord.
I will put my laws in their hearts, and
I will write them on their minds.

HEBREWS 10:16

~⌒~

Because God wanted to make the
unchanging nature of his purpose very
clear to the heirs of what was promised,
he confirmed it with an oath. God did
this so that, by two unchangeable things
in which it is impossible for God to lie,
we who have fled to take hold of the hope
offered to us may be greatly encouraged.

HEBREWS 6:17-18

~⌒~

Let us hold unswervingly to the hope we
profess, for he who promised is faithful.

HEBREWS 10:23

~⌒~

Pinky Swear

As kids, when someone made a promise, we liked to require lots of pomp and circumstance to make sure our bases were covered—a pinky swear, a handshake, a vow to sacrifice a favorite toy should the friend waiver in her commitment.

The difference between our version of promise and God's version is that his covenant is unshakable and eternal. Our actions don't change the solidity of his promises. He doesn't spit on his palm and ask for a high five, nor does he ask us to perform. The only ritual involved is the one of belief. If you are rusty on this, follow me. Lean into his love gently, faithfully, completely. You're covered.

I'm sorry for the times that I expect you to jump through hoops in order to satisfy my human version of promise. The truth is, I want to be freed from this way of thinking. Each day that I spend in your faithful presence leads me from doubt to belief. And your unconditional love covers me.

Right There

While paying for a DVD at a kiosk, I became aware of a person standing very close. My first feelings were (1) worry that my debit-card info was visible and (2) polite concern that I was making someone wait. When I turned to leave, I saw a tall, young woman who didn't look hurried or as if she were committing my PIN to memory.

When my awareness of God's presence is heightened, my first responses are similar. Either I'm afraid God will see my guarded secrets, or I'm concerned that God is tired of waiting for me to grow in faith. Eventually it sinks in... that despite what we've done or what we haven't done, God remains. And when we feel the spirit of fear come over us, all we have to do is look over our shoulder and remember that God is with us.

Release me from my worries about your getting too close, God. When I feel your presence, I want to rejoice in this security. Let me rest in your omnipresence and your grace. You are with me. I pray to realize what a gift this is every day.

Promises, Promises

Promises fall loosely from my lips when I'm in a hurry to discuss other important matters, like the length of my to-do list. Later, I end up digging through the debris of broken promises. My purpose then becomes more about damage control than living abundantly.

When we honor our commitments to others, to stewardship, to servanthood, to integrity, we can live with freedom and joy. May we pray for discernment before we speak promises. And when we indulge in one of the most popular sins of our times—overextending ourselves to the point of ineffectiveness—may we learn to ask for help.

God, silence my tongue if I am about to make a promise I cannot keep. Allow me to understand what I can take on and what I cannot. Grant me wisdom so that I may avoid the debris of my mistakes. Give me strength to be a person of honor. I long to model your eternal promises by the way I live this life.

Strong Finish

I'm in a recovery leg of my journey. My pace is slow, and I am trying to gather and conserve energy for the race I know will kick in up ahead. In the past, I mistook these times as moments of weakness or failure, but God intends for us to refuel. God wants us to lean on his might so that we are prepared and encouraged.

When you feel unable to keep going, you are ready for the recovery leg. In fact, most of us are well beyond ready before we realize God's desire to carry, direct, and renew us. God wants you to finish strong; he just didn't intend for you to run alone.

Lead me on, God. I am weary. I am tired. I find myself stumbling often. Forgive me for refusing to trust your strength early on. I wanted to run on my own terms. With each step, I'm learning how to give my pace over to your peace and my race over to your restoration.

Tell Me More

I like to know that happy times are happening and that people are achieving goals, finding joy, and reaching for their personal callings. When I read of someone's taking a leap of faith, my heart rises with the arc of the story and beats with possibility. Don't we all want these bits of inspiration?

When we catch ourselves listening more carefully to our inner voices of doubt than to God's steady words of encouragement, it is time to ask for a new way to hear his promises. God gives us many stories of good news and is the author of *the* good news. Are you ready to listen?

Tell me more about the goodness of your will and your ways. Give me an ear for all that is wise and worthy. May I ignore that which is false, harmful, and unrighteous. Where I have become lazy in my quest for honor and honesty, inspire me with role models. Give me the courage to stand strong so that my life declares your good news.

Wishes and Dreams

I've closed my eyes to blow out many candles and have made many wishes. Those wishes became dreams; some eventually turned into the stepping stones of goals. I walk forward with my sights set on how I'd like life to be.

Our wishes and dreams are important. They often rise up to lead us toward our true calling and purpose. But when our hope is grounded in the security of God's faithfulness, we can do more than make a wish, we can lift up a prayer and know that it is heard.

God, reveal to me those dreams that are of your plan and purpose for me. Thank you for those moments when I feel the wonder of a future hope. I know that the wishes that do come true are reflections of your brilliant life-giving light.

This Life Protected By...

I house-sat for a friend who had a security system. I'm used to just unlocking a dead bolt, so I was a little flustered when I had to enter a series of numbers quickly. If I was off by one digit or reversed the order or paused too long between entries, an alarm sounded.

We can be thankful that God does not require such precise steps in order to gain entrance to his presence and protection. When we are his, we can rest in the security of his shelter—no passcode needed. If we are unable to connect with God, it is time to look at what personally keeps us from entering his presence. The door is open.

Thank you, thank you for being so accessible.
My heart had high walls built around it until
you showed me the comfort and character of
unconditional love. I can stop protecting my
heart because you are there to watch over me.

Take a Vow

Your soul experiences a supernatural joy when the vow of faith is taken. It makes you want to stand before friends, family, and strangers and declare your undying love for never-ending Love. You'll find yourself looking for ways to show and tell others "I love because he first loved me."

Committed faith calls you to move, speak, and act out of gratitude. Your sorrows and celebrations are shaped by the very moment you took your vow and left solitary struggle in exchange for a life connected to and shared by God. The rewards of a shared life await you.

I commit to so many people, obligations, and even struggles. Lead me to the altar of renewed faith commitment. I want to know you personally, intimately, and completely. Thank you for not only promising a forever I can believe in, but also walking with me from this day forward.

Searching

Shelves of knickknacks overflowed. I kept walking. Delicate jewelry sparkled beneath the glass of a display case. I moved on. Candles in shades of autumn gave off scents of a Thanksgiving feast. I continued my search. An unassuming tray of charms featuring words of inspiration rested on the counter. "That's it!" I said and purchased several treasures for my friend.

If you have times when you feel like you are wandering through life, your desire to find God's best will lead you. Even when you don't know what you're searching for, the treasures you'll discover will be just what you need, long for, and are made for.

*I shouldn't be surprised by the many moments,
connections, and wonders you bring into my life,
but I am. May I never get so lost in my search
that I don't notice the treasures that are of your
purpose for me. When I say, "That's it!" after a
long time of unknowing, may I give thanks.*

Unchanging

A friend I haven't seen in a long time e-mailed me to share that he had a dream in which I had dyed my hair a different color. In the dream he was trying to tell me nicely that even though I looked good in my new, interesting style, I shouldn't try to be like anyone else.

The details of the dream weren't accurate, but the essence was important. It is tempting to want to emulate a style, goal, or vision for life that we have witnessed in another. But God doesn't call us to be like someone else; he calls us to become who we are intended to be. Our preferences may come and go, but our identity in Christ is unchanging.

Lord, how am I trying to be someone that I am not? How have I wasted vital energy on trying to change myself in superficial ways? You do not call me to change who I am; you call me to the great I AM and promise transformation through your grace and mercy. When I stray, allow me to protect the me that is your child.

Grace

Words for Grace

When [Barnabas] arrived and saw the
evidence of the grace of God, he was
glad and encouraged them all to remain
true to the Lord with all their hearts.

ACTS 11:23

Now I commit you to God and to the
word of his grace, which can build
you up and give you an inheritance
among all those who are sanctified.

ACTS 20:32

Where sin increased, grace
increased all the more.

ROMANS 5:20

By the grace God has given me, I laid
a foundation as an expert builder, and
someone else is building on it.

1 CORINTHIANS 3:10

By the grace of God I am what I am, and
his grace to me was not without effect. No,
I worked harder than all of them—yet not
I, but the grace of God that was with me.

1 CORINTHIANS 15:10

All this is for your benefit, so that the grace that
is reaching more and more people may cause
thanksgiving to overflow to the glory of God.

2 CORINTHIANS 4:15

Just as you excel in everything—in faith,
in speech, in knowledge, in complete
earnestness and in your love for us—see
that you also excel in this grace of giving.

2 CORINTHIANS 8:7

And God is able to make all grace
abound to you, so that in all things at
all times, having all that you need, you
will abound in every good work.

2 CORINTHIANS 9:8

Witness

We are witnesses to God's love and grace daily. Let's grab on to these confirmations of all that our Creator is and will be for us and for the world. When we are exposed to bad news or we find ourselves serving a slice of gossip or believing a rumor, it also becomes our opportunity to go the way of goodness—to listen only to the still small voice that clearly guides us with truth.

Grace happens minute by minute. If you are not seeing it in action throughout your day, then it is time to put it into practice. Share with others the great gift you experience as a child of God.

In many ways you reveal your sweet forgiveness
and power to make the broken whole. Help me
to express your love through kindness, justice,
compassion, purity, and the willingness to
be a reflection of your abundant grace.

Foundation of Grace

Grace—how can something that sounds so soft, comfortable, and giving be so solid? When people engage in the details of dogma or the arguments of theology, I find the interaction initially exciting and motivating. I want to understand God and faith in deeper ways. But after a while, debates make me dizzy. I want to lie down on something solid.

Ah, back to grace. It is my truth and hope and belief. My life has been wrapped in it, covered by it, and restored because of it. When I stand firmly on the rock of grace, the questions can keep coming, but I rest in what I know to be true.

*Opinions, public forum, and issue debates help me
define my faith in stronger terms and convictions.
But, God, I'm so thankful that I can take refuge
in your grace. When I face doubts or questions
or even my own curiosity, I know that I stand
firm on a foundation of your good grace.*

Portion Control

We live in a world caught between a sense of super-sized entitlement and a belief in repentance via portion control. The view of grace can be similar. Some view it as an open-ended license to do as they please. Others view it as a restricted blessing distributed based on merit. Either image distorts the beauty of God's great grace.

There is no human-crafted formula that will figure out how grace works, how it covers hurts and sins and shattered hearts. God's grace has us covered in proportion to what we need. As consumers, we can ask how much is too much. As Christians we need only say "Your grace is sufficient" and "Thank you" on our way to a richer, deeper faith.

I'm sorry for the times I acted as though your grace was there for me as backup so that I could do what I wanted. I don't want to take it for granted. I want to experience the beauty, the depth, the joy, and the miracle of the grace gift.

Pass It Along

We are so fortunate to know grace firsthand, but it isn't meant to stop with us. Try committing a week of passing grace on to others. Anyone and everyone. The slow clerk at the market, the lost driver who keeps veering, the friend who is worried about the same thing yet again, the family member quick with hurtful comments, the child who makes mistakes. Show them grace by responding with patience, understanding, and empathy.

Experience grace from God. Model it for others. And extend it to yourself. We can be so tough and critical when it comes to our own looks, choices, gifts, and efforts. View your life through the forgiving lens of grace, and every situation will look fresh and optimistic.

I stand in your forgiveness and mercy each day, but I forget to share this freedom with others through my actions and responses. Remind me of the times I have received grace from friends and family and strangers. I know that I can become self-focused all day long. Turn my attention to the grace that abounds, and may I be a part of it today.

God Doesn't Leave

I've had friends float in and out of my life. I've lost loved ones either through death or distance. Some relationships were harder to let go of than others, because the void made me feel alone. It isn't easy to be left out or left behind. We learn this early on in the politics of playgrounds.

When the heart feels abandoned and hope bends from the weight of loneliness, we can turn our worried faces toward God. We can cling to his hem and hold tightly. When our tears are brushed away by fingers of compassion and our shoulders lovingly patted by the hands that shaped our lives, we know that Grace never leaves us behind.

I want to get lost in the folds of unconditional love and unrestricted comfort. You don't ask why I'm so upset. You've witnessed my hurt, my loss, and my silly woes. You never judge the importance of what I bring to you. It all matters. Besides, you know that I am here today to remind myself that you are here always.

When Things Aren't Things

If we keep the harvest of faith such as grace, love, compassion, kindness, etc. as lofty by-products of belief, we miss the chance to express them tangibly. We let ourselves off the hook of an active faith. Faith without works is saved by grace, but it becomes a lifeless faith and ends up looking far different from the image of God.

Dig into grace, love, compassion, kindness, and forgiveness, and pull out something that the world or even one single person can relate to. Give these blessings dimension and weight. How? Share a meal. Make a donation. Take the hand of someone who needs healing. Give away some "thing" that matters to you. Help load groceries for a fragile stranger. Things are so much more than things when they are used to express a living, active, abundant faith.

What is right in front of me that I need to fix, give away, pass along, lift up, release, or transform into something useful? How can my hands serve today? How can my strength bring relief to someone? What can I give that is indeed sacrifice so that my discomfort is turned into the comfort of another? Help me give my faith a workout.

Wantin' Ways

When we see the even better version of the techno-gadget we just bought, it is difficult but important to remember that our truest wants are met by God's grace alone—if we'll release them, that is! As tightly as we hold on to the material world as our source of identity and power, we are to hold on to God's truth and purpose for us.

The more we let go, the more grace abounds. The more we step out in faith without the safety net of résumé success, the more we sense the power of grace. Our eyes might wander to the next big thing, but may our hearts look upward at the one true thing.

It is by your grace that I move forward, feel love, experience blessing, survive trials, and see beyond doubt to hope. My false needs come and go as quickly as commercials, but my authentic, life-transforming longings will only be filled by the bounty of a faithful heart.

The Way It Should Be

My tribute to God goes a bit like this: "I falter. You recover. I betray good intentions. You redeem hearts. I fear. You calm. I give up. You show me the way. I distrust. You remain. I cheat. You offer real answers. I backpedal. You inspire me to press on."

Do you have a similar ongoing pattern? Did you know that this is a good thing? We have every opportunity to try, to dare, to live fully because when our shortcomings are strongest or our need for extra help the greatest, God's power is at work and on display in our lives. We are walking, talking billboards for God's grace and hope. Repeat after me, "I am weak, but you are strong." Yes, Jesus loves us…and may the world know it.

When I credit you with my life and life's strength, others will see your glory in my missteps or my victories. I need not worry about the outcome because you are shaping it carefully. I want people to know that I am weak but you are strong.

Testify

If we understand what faith is all about, we will become expert witnesses to God's grace. When we get that it is not our strength but God's that ushers us through each day, then we can speak of this truth in the court of everyday people. Whether we're with those who know or don't know God, our offerings of faith, encouragement, God's peace, and wisdom should not vary.

Life is hard. Let's face it. But let's face it by walking faithfully. And when we do, there will be no other explanation for why we are content, sane, kind, whole, forgiving, trusting, and eager to testify as an eyewitness to grace.

God, I have hesitated to share what I know with others. I don't trust myself to get it right or to reflect you sufficiently. How can I...I am only me? But you don't need me to fix everything or every person I encounter. You call me to the stand to share my story, my version of one life dependent on grace. This I can do...with your help, of course.

Back to Freedom

I've grown accustomed to fallback sources of freedom that come with worldly credentials: power, financing, might, escape, approval, security of the masses. I want them backing my every move, because what if life doesn't turn out the way I planned? What if there's illness? What if there's loss of work? What if there's war? What if there are unknowns?

Every time we greet the sun and step into a new day, there are unknowns. But when we lean into the certainty of our all-knowing God, we rest in absolute freedom.

Life can feel like a free fall. Help me release my grip on the world's securities so that I look only to the safety net of grace. You don't keep me from the "what ifs," but when I listen to your leading, you guide me through the unknowns.

Direction

Words for Direction

Direct me in the path of your commands,
for there I find delight.

PSALM 119:35

~~~~~

You guide me with your counsel,
and afterward you will take me into glory.

PSALM 73:24

~~~~~

Show me your ways, O LORD,
teach me your paths;
guide me in your truth and teach me,
for you are God my Savior,
and my hope is in you all day long.

PSALM 25:4-5

~~~~~

Into your hands I commit my spirit;
redeem me, O LORD, the God of truth.

PSALM 31:5

Teach me your way, O LORD;
lead me in a straight path.

PSALM 27:11

The path of life leads upward for the wise.

PROVERBS 15:24

Open Eyes

Some days I feel like I am sleepwalking. A haze clouds my mind and heart as I make my way through the maze of scheduled tasks or conversations. And then a comment, a thought, or a scene will capture my attention. I've been missing out on the gift of a new day, a series of possibilities, and a string of moments that God designed for me to experience, to witness, and to hold in heart and mind.

Some "pay attention" moments might be deemed unremarkable by others, but to me they are windows into God's heart for my life. I see his humor in a child's silly joke, his wisdom in a friend's counsel, and his love for me when I come across a well-timed verse from Scripture that speaks to my immediate situation.

Pull me out of the fog of routine so I can witness the wonders that I used to pass by on my way to more busyness. Open my eyes to every moment. Allow me to see the people and the possibilities and the path you carve out for me each day.

In Charge

With my cell phone on, my e-mail filling the screen, and my mental list of duties for the day, I feel slightly powerful. I'm in charge of the moment and, if I stay on task, maybe even in control of the day.

The world would have us think we are in control of our days and our lives. It becomes easy to think of God as a good friend rather than the all-knowing Creator who sees and shapes the big picture and the fine details. Eventually interruptions and disconnections change the course of even the best plans. Consider these disruptions blessings—gentle reminders that we're not in charge but are loved, noticed, and guided by the One who is.

You are my only power source. You made me so that I could use my abilities, my mind, and my life to bring you glory. When I start to think that I control people, details, and my future, remind me—gently please— that I'm not in charge of life. I'm in your charge.

Formula

Most parents wish their children came with a manual. For our own lives, we know that's ridiculous thinking…yet how many of us are secretly hoping that we'll come upon a formula for success and happiness?

There isn't a secret code that will fulfill the universal quest for significance. You personally *know* the Maker of mankind, the Genius behind gravity, and the Inventor of starfish and eyelashes; the only formula you need is: one (you) + one (God) equals relationship. Profound and simple—these are the characteristics of a great truth.

Okay, I'll confess that I've been hoping that formula would appear. I was trying to figure out my life without the power of faith. I got caught up in human answers. God, protect me from my own desires so that I can rest in your desires for me.

Awake and Alive

How often do we live our lives without watching for glimpses of God and his wonders? When we place our feet on the floor and begin a new day with a stretch, let's add in a short prayer to be fully aware of the One who is fully alive and in charge and in love with life. Let this prayer shape our day, our mood, our outlook, and our hope.

Let's awaken our hearts, minds, and spirits so that we don't waste the sacred gift of a day. Even a regular day has its miracle moments, if we'll just open our eyes in time to be a witness to the life God is shaping for us, in us, around us, and through us daily.

Creator, show me what it is to be among the fully awake, the fully vested, the fully living. Release me from the numbness of routine, and recharge my spirit with your love. I want to see your beauty and purpose and power in this life I live.

Typecasting

Am I an introvert or an extrovert? Do I lean toward type-A personality characteristics? Do I have the "it" factor? Am I more of a behind-the-scenes person or a leader? What credentials do I bring to the table? The answers to the questions aren't about who I am; they are about finding a label that the world can use for quick acceptance or dismissal.

Thank goodness God doesn't try to force us into stereotypes. He's the Maker of the individual. There is, however, a label worth aspiring to—child of God—and it requires only that we become the one of a kind he created us to be.

God, I know you have great plans for me and provide me with what I need. Teach me to stop trying to fit into the world's categories when I can stand with courage and confidence in the identity and faith you blessed me with even before I was born.

Cliffhanger

Purpose is like a huge canyon. Something one could get lost in, fall into, or spend many hours staring at with amazement and uncertainty. Are we meant to just get to the other side? Should we repel down to the canyon floor? If we started out in the wrong direction on a shaky overhang, would someone pull us back to safety?

Even if we don't personally ask "What is my purpose here in this life?" we are still reminded of the question by our fellow journey travelers. The good news is that we aren't standing here alone. God is our guide into it, through it, or around it—depending on our particular purpose. (And for the record, he will pull you back to safety.)

So many unanswered questions. I want to know my purpose. I want to stand at the edge of the canyon and feel freedom rather than fear, possibility rather than panic, direction rather than danger. I might close my eyes sometimes, but I'm ready, God. Lead me to it.

Keep Walking

When the path gets rocky, remain steady. When the hills become steep, start climbing. When bystanders question your direction, stay the course. When bumps feel like mountains, step higher. When you are thirsty and hungry, watch for sustenance. When you are lonely and doubting, ask for help. When your body aches, lean on the strength of the Spirit. When the road is cast in darkness, shed light on it.

When you look behind you and don't recognize the path and you look ahead and it, too, is foreign, keep walking. You're almost there.

God, there are so many unknowns. I'd love to step onto a path and know without a doubt that there's not any other way to go. I'm absolutely right. Instead, the faith journey requires me to give my path over to you and know that you are God. The way of truth. The way of life. The way of love. And the way I should go. Absolutely.

So Very Green

That grass over there is lush, thick, and glossy, and the green is so deep it bears a halo of blue. My friend's gifts and abilities are so colorful and remarkable I can't help but stare at his journey and question why I didn't follow a similar route. Sure, my gifts are completely different, and yes I'd have to give up my passions to follow his, but still...

Here's the truth: the grass is always going to seem greener on the other side. But it really is all about the lighting. When you illuminate your own portion of purpose, it is brilliant too. Spend time observing it and being grateful. It's quite incredible on your side of life.

Why has it taken me so long to see the beauty of my own life? I've taken for granted those strengths you have given me. I've squandered time and my resources by ignoring your leading. I'm ready to celebrate the wonder of this life you have entrusted to me. I return it to you and ask to be a part of the miracle.

Test Kitchen

All the cooking shows these days remind us how the wonders of a good meal represent those of a good life. It's about the pleasure of the senses, the ingredients that make the ordinary sumptuous, and the opportunity of creating something worth savoring.

Go to the test kitchen for your life. Add inspired ingredients for new flavor like new friends, adventure, trying a hobby, trust in yourself, new perspective about your job, whatever has been missing in your batches. A sprinkle of possibility, a dash of insight, and a cup of faith mixed with plenty of prayer—a life of meaning is in the works!

Your love is poured out over my life. I want to serve you by making the most of my days. I know that there are many ingredients you've brought my way that I've been reluctant to try. I don't want to be afraid to add richness. I want to savor every moment.

Healing

Words for Healing

Jacob made a vow, saying, "If God will
be with me and will watch over me on
this journey I am taking and will give
me food to eat and clothes to wear so
that I return safely to my father's house,
then the LORD will be my God."

GENESIS 28:20-21

O LORD my God, I called to you for help
and you healed me.

PSALM 30:2

Rise up and help us;
redeem us because of your unfailing love.

PSALM 44:26

Restore us, O God;
make your face shine upon us,
that we may be saved.

PSALM 80:3

⁓

The LORD protects the simplehearted;
when I was in great need, he saved me.

PSALM 116:6

⁓

Pleasant words are a honeycomb,
sweet to the soul and healing to the bones.

PROVERBS 16:24

⁓

Heal me, O LORD, and I will be healed;
save me and I will be saved,
for you are the one I praise.

JEREMIAH 17:14

⁓

Be Here

I've been asking God to be with me a lot lately, to wrap me in his full presence, and to help me feel closer to normal. I want healing from soul to bone, from mind to skin, from prayer to truth. My focus on this is all-consuming.

Thirst for mercy comes on so violently when want and worry leave us stripped of all other resources. God must wish we'd seek to be filled and satiated before we stand in drought's ruin. Go to his mercy today. Give yourself over to God as a daily practice and preserve the reserve of your soul's only source of renewal.

I want to mend the parched places of my mind and spirit on my own terms or at least when it is more convenient. Today I come to you with the hurts I recognize and those I have ignored. May your mercy rush over me, and may it bring healing.

On the Bridge

From brokenness to wholeness is a great distance. I've stood here before, but this time it is more daunting. Honestly, I can't even see what this situation looks like on the other side of pain. What if there is a drop-off somewhere between hurt and healing? A jagged cliff where one false hope can leave me tumbling?

When we face the chasm of illness or failing or despair, the restoration might not always be visible, but God's hope, grace, mercy, faithfulness, and love are shaping it even now. When the abyss is vast, God's bridge of healing is rising up. Take a step forward; it will hold you up.

I'm afraid to step forward in this experience. I can't manage the unknown without the assurance of your presence. Your healing does not require me to "manage" anything. I know this too. Help me release this desire to control every detail, Lord. I'd rather walk with faith, even into the unknown, than without it.

Sutures

When we walk through trials, the stings and the pains we feel might seem familiar. We might be facing a different hardship, but wounds from long ago can be reopened if we haven't given them over to God's healing. When we nurse them with our own version of healing—self-help solutions, a change of job or address, burying the pain—we will feel the pain afresh eventually.

God takes our emotional and spiritual injuries and seals them with sutures of promise, mercy, and understanding. Exchange your version of remedy for God's authentic healing.

I hurt so deeply. I keep revisiting this pain. Each time, I think I have suffered a different wound caused by a new weapon. But this one is not new for me. I've kept it open and buried by my ignorance and stubbornness. Mend me, Lord. I want true healing.

Soul Shattering

Like a lip quivering, the soul expresses the first tremors of fear. What is shaking the foundation you have built your security on? Is it a loss of a loved one? An uncertain prognosis in life or health? A crisis of faith? An unexplainable fear that takes over?

Sometimes we don't know what causes our souls to shatter. It might not be for you to ever discover—that is a difficult truth to accept. But hold tightly to the peace of what you do know...*who* will put the pieces back together. And he will.

God, I can't stop shaking on the inside. I want to feel whole and complete. Take the fragments of my spirit and piece me together in your time and in your grace. May I stand on the unshakable ground of hope so that the world can see your strength.

Eyes on Jesus

I've been waiting for healing so long that I've started to watch for something else. Any distraction will do. Like an impatient tourist on my way to a paradise, I begin to think the desolate stops on the way represent the destination, and I become discouraged.

The wonder of the destination will be lost on us if we don't realize the meaning of each time of waiting. When the view is dismal, it is because we have missed the point of the stop—it is a time to focus our eyes ever so closely on Jesus.

This time has a purpose in my life. I am thankful that it causes me, compels me, to seek out your face. There is peace and comfort in that face. Love cradles me even when I am resistant. Beauty envelops me even when the view is not what I signed up to see. Don't let me be tempted by distraction when your beauty is so clearly what I am meant to notice.

Better than New

Americans are obsessed with overhauling houses, bodies, cars, and lives. If we had enough money or the right opportunity, wouldn't we all love a makeover of some kind? Why then do we often deny the freely given transformations of faith—from damaged to mended, from dead to living, from ignorant to wise, from blind to sighted?

Maybe our vision of remodel is far too limited. We want a new look, a new ride, or a new size. God is ready to give us a better-than-new life. What are we waiting for?

I've been longing for a touch-up when you are offering a complete exchange of old for new. I carry around sins, hurts, regrets, and shame while wishing for a house with a swimming pool. God, help me grow up so that I can experience a life, a purpose, a faith that is better than new.

God Only Knows

When nobody is watching, God is there. When you have been abandoned, cut by words, torn by abuse…God sees it, and he weeps for the loss of justice, innocence, and peace. In the darkest moment, you are not left to bear the suffering alone.

God provides the strength you need right where you are. God has a plan in motion to repair your soul. He will bring you comfort, he will lead you to refuge, he will show you the tears he shed that moment when you thought you were lost forever.

I am so thankful that I don't have to stand as a solo witness to the pain. I have been afraid to release the wound because I wanted there to be a record of the injustice and the reason for my brokenness. But you were there. You are here. And you share my sorrow because you love me. This love is the reason for my healing.

Over the Counter

Last year I had a sinus headache that turned to infection. However, I was busy with work, so I kept hoping an over-the-counter medication would correct the problem. Well, my real problem was my faulty thinking. One plane ride later, my head felt like it was in a vise, but my mind finally got the message: This problem isn't going away—get the antibiotics.

Have you ever done the same with a spiritual problem? Is there a reoccurring sin you try to fix with mere self-determination or positive thinking? It remains, doesn't it? And it causes more pain each time. Stop reaching for over-the-counter solutions when your painful sin needs supernatural healing.

The pain is deep. My sin is beginning to consume me.
I wanted an easy out, and the truth is, you offer one.
You have offered to take this from me. My journey
won't be simple, but your answer is. Here. Take it.

What Can You Make of This?

Jigsaw puzzles may have caused a problem. They provide us with a finite number of pieces and a picture of the end result. With a little time and patience, everything comes together. But when it comes to pieces of our lives, the fragments that follow heartbreak or breakdowns, everything doesn't add up to the picture we have stuck in our heads.

This isn't about giving up, but giving *over*. Hand the pieces to God. He knows what the big picture looks like. Are you clutching a piece right now? Have you tried to force it to fit your image of healing? Let go. God is trying to make something wonderful.

God, what can you make of all these pieces? I've been trying to force my emotions along so that I could say I was better. I wanted everyone around me to see the picture of someone who had moved past the pain. But I'm stuck, and I'm tired of this false image. I can't wait to see what you are going to make of this life of mine.

Compassion

Words for Compassion

You care for the land and water it;
yet you enrich it abundantly.
The streams of God are filled with water
to provide the people with grain,
for so you have ordained it.

Psalm 65:9

The Lord is gracious and compassionate,
slow to anger and rich in love.
The Lord is good to all;
he has compassion on all he has made.

Psalm 145:8-9

Do not judge, and you will not be
judged. Do not condemn, and you
will not be condemned. Forgive,
and you will be forgiven.

Luke 6:37

Be kind and compassionate to one
another, forgiving each other, just
as in Christ God forgave you.

EPHESIANS 4:32

As God's chosen people, holy and dearly
loved, clothe yourselves with compassion,
kindness, humility, gentleness and patience.

COLOSSIANS 3:12

Finally, all of you, live in harmony with
one another; be sympathetic, love as
brothers, be compassionate and humble.

1 PETER 3:8

Past Ourselves Is God

We try and try and try to make things right. And the next time our lives need fixing, we'll likely try again and stumble. I have news that I'm hoping you'll consider wonderfully freeing—we aren't meant to fix our own lives. When we fail at this task, there is a perfectly good reason. Or better said, there is a perfect God reason.

He is the perfecter of our lives and our faith. At the point where our ability ends, God awaits. Here we discover the significance of compassion—here we extend grace to ourselves as we fall into God's unconditional love.

When I say I'm done with trying, I mean it! Well, at least this time I mean it. I want to give over my circumstances to you so that I can personally, intimately experience the point where I end and you continue for eternity. I want to be free of my limitations.

Long Vision

"Jesus had compassion on them and touched their eyes. Immediately they received their sight and followed him" (Matthew 20:34). How has God healed you? How has his touch expanded your vision of life or love or purpose? When your eyes were opened to the resurrected life, did you immediately follow him?

The compassion of Christ changes everything—our view, our horizon, and our future. When we respond to the touch of healing with a desire to follow his ways of mercy, we will have our eyes opened to purpose and calling.

God, you have opened my eyes to your compassion, to your promises, and to new life in you. I want to leave behind the limited purpose I had been walking in before my encounter with your saving grace. Show me what is next. I am watching, I am following, and I am believing.

Cultivating a Compassionate Life

It takes a lot of planning and care to grow a bountiful garden, which probably explains why I don't have one. How much more plotting and attention is required to nurture an abundant life! I can forego the backyard vegetables, but I long for a life that produces a good, decent harvest that honors God.

We know the Master Gardener, but we are also called to tend to our spiritual growth. One of the most important crops we can raise is that of compassion. The more you plant in the hearts of others, the more that will grow in your own life. It's plantin' season.

Show me how to sow compassion. Alleviate my own anxieties and anger so that I can demonstrate your love to those I encounter—stranger or friend. My faith softens my heart; may this become the fertile ground in which compassion takes root.

Slow to Anger

There is no favoritism in God's kingdom. He is fond of all he has made. He has compassion and unconditional love for all his children. I love the idea of God being slow to anger and rich in love (Psalm 145:8-9). It is such an interesting pairing—anger and love; think how often we choose to express one over the other.

If we can adopt a "slow to anger" policy in our interactions, there will be a much better chance for love to take hold and shape our relationships.

I envision anger on one side of a seesaw and love on the other. God, how often do I try to sway a situation toward anger, when the shift should be toward your wealth of love? Don't let me slide toward indifference when a heart of compassion can anchor me to your faithfulness.

Empathize Me

Sympathy brings us flowers, it cries for us from a distance, and it keeps us in mind. But empathy sits with us in the sorrow or the difficulty. Empathy connects to the shared truth and questions in a person's journey. Empathy doesn't mind red eyes and messy hair and times of silence.

Being empathetic takes sacrifice. Often you must go to uncomfortable depths of your own spirit and sorrow to reach the source waters of empathy. But when you get there, you can draw from God's compassion, rest in uncertainty, and share the burden of another. When you get there, you get a glimpse of God's great love.

Give me a heart beyond my own heart. I get too caught up in my opinions and my life circumstances. Still my thoughts, turn my focus to the deep need of another. Help me have patience to just sit with another person's pain...even when answers seem distant, even when it is uncomfortable.

Judge Not

I like to say that I am antijudgmental and pro-grace. Yet I still find this unattractive defense mechanism interfering with my days. I use judgment as a protective shield against the possible criticism of others—a first-strike strategy. "They can't hurt me because I can list five things wrong with them." No, this isn't logical, but it is human.

Judgment fills our thoughts quickly. It takes over our actions and responses. It leaves no room for understanding and compassion. It's helpful to have the image of a courtroom judge to associate with the word. Each time you judge another and place yourself above another child of God, you sentence that person and yourself to a life devoid of compassion.

Lord, lead me away from the chambers of judgment.
When I get on my high horse and want to place
value on a person or their behavior, remind me
what I would be without you and your grace.
Fill my heart with unconditional compassion,
and help me leave the big judgments to you.

Compassion Sense

What's your style? Dramatic? Practical? Whimsical? Servanthood? Didn't you know there's a dress code for servanthood? Really, it's more of a uniform: "Clothe yourselves with compassion, kindness, humility, gentleness and patience" (Colossians 3:12).

Each day when you reach for the right attire, don't forget the spiritual clothing you'll need to love others, extend grace, be used by God, and get noticed for the statement you make by your faith accessories.

I stand before you naked, my own nature stripped away so that I can be clothed by character that reflects you. You give us all unique personal styles through our own callings and purposes, and then you add to it with the fabric of compassion, kindness, humility, gentleness, and patience. May we wear it well.

Acts of Forgiveness

We've all seen the bumper stickers encouraging random acts of kindness. I'm thinking that maybe a better way to change the world would be through intentional acts of forgiveness. Our culture has become very blasé about the importance of asking for and extending forgiveness.

Think how your day and attitude would change if you started each morning with the intention of forgiving anyone and anything. Is your mind already drafting a list of things you couldn't possibly forgive? That's why this must be intentional. If we lean on our own measure of justice, we'll never adopt God's measure of grace. Go forth and forgive.

I forget to go to you with the burden of my sins and my weaknesses. It has been even longer since I asked another person for forgiveness, even though there have been many circumstances when it would've been the right thing. Lord, help me to step beyond my pride so that I can walk intentionally toward a life that gives and seeks forgiveness.

Tenderness

I used to watch my mother tenderize meat by pounding it or poking it with a fork. I must admit, I was a skeptic. Wouldn't such force harden the piece of beef or pork? But it always worked, and I became a believer (and a happy eater).

While many hearts have been hardened by the blows of disappointment, I would state the case for the power of trials and suffering to change the consistency of our hearts for the better. But only through God, and only with the power of prayer and grace. Our sadness and tough times can be transformed into tenderness and compassion. Become a believer.

God, I give you these hardened places of my spirit and mind. I've closed off my ability to nurture my wounds. They need the balm of your care. Tenderize my heart. Melt away the fear that keeps me from reaching out to others or from expressing my feelings. Please, Lord…turn this hardened life into one that can easily be shaped and seasoned by love.

From a Distance

Our computer home page reveals news and images of brutality, war, and pain. Some situations are far away, and that makes us feel a bit safer even if we are saddened by word of trouble for any nation, any people. We say "Isn't it a shame," or "God, do something!" but do we take on God's heart of compassion for these distant sorrows?

It's risky to move beyond a general concern to an involved compassion. You never know what God might call you to do should you invest your heart and prayers in the plight of another child of God. Remember, from where God is—in us and among us—the distance between you and them is nonexistent. Do something.

How can I help someone I don't know who is so far away? I know that you nudge me to begin with the person next to me. They have needs too. Yet what have I done to show them unconditional love? I will make the decision to stop passively viewing hardship so that I can begin living in an active state of compassion, for those near or far.

Fulfillment

Words for Fulfillment

From heaven the LORD looks down
and sees all mankind;
from his dwelling place he watches
all who live on earth—
he who forms the hearts of all,
who considers everything they do.

PSALM 33:13-15

How can I repay the LORD
for all his goodness to me?
I will lift up the cup of salvation
and call on the name of the LORD.
I will fulfill my vows to the LORD
in the presence of all his people.

PSALM 116:12-14

The LORD will fulfill [his purpose] for me;
your love, O LORD, endures forever—
do not abandon the works of your hands.

PSALM 138:8

When I fed them, they were satisfied;
when they were satisfied,
they became proud;
then they forgot me.

HOSEA 13:6

⁓

I always thank God for you because of
his grace given you in Christ Jesus. For
in him you have been enriched in every
way—in all your speaking and in all
your knowledge—because our testimony
about Christ was confirmed in you.

1 CORINTHIANS 1:4-6

⁓

God's Dependent

When we consider that God is our provider for *everything*, we also need to consider that we are dependent upon him for *everything*. If God had to file with the IRS, he'd do quite well. Each of us is a dependent living under his roof and relying on his care and feeding.

The truly amazing part is that our complete dependence on God is our pass to freedom and fulfillment. We can step forward without worries about our survival or purpose. These might still sneak into our thoughts, but we are free to let them go. You, me, our neighbors, our family members… we are listed under his charge.

Grant me dependence, Lord. That's right. I'm glad to be a dependent in your household. You care for me, you plot out my days, you deliver goodness to my doorstep, and you revive my soul. My hunger for a place in this world is fulfilled with the home of plenty in your heart.

It's Beyond Me

I've told God so many times that I am not up to the task of handling my current life stresses. I've expressed my anger about these pressures along with suggestions as to how they can be resolved. You see, I had plans, and this latest glitch was not in them. Have you ever had your perfect life plans interrupted?

I've figured out that this point of venting and possibly whining can be a good sign. It means we're finally getting close to the solution. When we get that life management is beyond our ability, then we're ready for God to take over. And do you know what? That life plan we had…it's nothing compared to what's in store for us with God at the helm.

God, lead me past this point. Beyond what I can handle is the strength, your strength, that I am supposed to rest in. Of course my life goes haywire sometimes. It is because I was not created to manage it on my own. Make this the life you intended for me. I give it over to you completely.

Satisfaction or Fulfillment

Do you look upon situations with a sense of satisfaction or dissatisfaction? Do people and results tend to disappoint you? What do you think you are waiting for to truly ease the void and the expectations? What blocks you from receiving joy and fulfillment? So many questions! But these do lead somewhere.

If you don't examine your barriers to an abundant life, it becomes easy to blame other people or God for your problems, worries, disappointments, and mistakes. I believe fulfillment comes only when we are faithful to truth. Discover what holds you back, and give that truth over to God. He transforms the fragments of disappointment into the whole of contentment.

How long have I held back from a good, full life, Lord? I hold on to the failings of myself and those around me as an excuse. I lift them up and say, "See…this is all life is." But you take these and say they are not my truth, but they are the proof that I need you in order to be complete.

Zero-Interest Loan

Are you ever flat-out amazed at the life you're leading? Amazement can happen even if your daily activities won't make the cover of a "living large" magazine. When you awaken to the incredible miracles at play, you open your eyes to the deeper value of your purpose; you become motivated to serve the gift of fulfilling each day's potential.

This extraordinary journey is yours to embrace and cherish and savor and live. We could never really repay God for the gift of life, but every day we devote to living out our exceptional, irreplaceable, significant, personal paths, we get a bit closer to making good on the loan.

Sometimes I try to repay you for this life with guilt-induced actions. I want to do my best from a place of gratitude. I want to serve my purpose for being with every day I am given. God, the idea that you have ordained this life for me, just me, as one of significance is all I need to inspire my next move…out of sincere gratitude.

Did That!

Checklists give us a sense of control and present finish lines for big and small accomplishments. I feel the power as I scratch off mundane things like washing my car, paying the mortgage, scheduling an appointment, etc. We tend to gravitate toward those solutions that seem simple: "Ten ways to improve your life," "Five steps to a new job."

God doesn't work this way. We're given some clear guidelines for living (like "Be kind to one another"), but it isn't for us to know how everything will unfold. Keep moving forward in faith and in God's will. Fulfillment will come. If you desperately need the thrill of a checklist, write on your heart every day to be faithful in your pursuit of God's purpose.

I like to know what is coming, and I like to see clear steps toward the end result. It is probably from the days of college-course syllabi or multiple-choice tests. God, help me keep my focus on that one line, "Be faithful," and may I close each day with an offering of prayer and a very clear "Did that!"

Drop the Cash

If I made a movie loosely based on the end of life, it would have a scene with a bank robber getting caught mid-heist. He (or she) stands with a look of utter surprise as a magnified voice says, "Drop the money and come on out with your hands up."

While our end might not play out like this, I can guarantee that we will have to drop whatever material possessions are in our clutches. We will hopefully release our hold on things of this world eagerly. But are you willing to start letting go now? If you are clinging to material gain for your fulfillment, I have some advice: Drop the cash, and walk forward with your hands wide open to receive the life God has for you.

I confess, I do find my material blessings to be more than a comfort; they've become my security and my chance to say, "I have arrived." Give me a heart for a life richer than riches and more valuable than valuables. May I cling only to the wealth of spiritual treasures so that when my time does come... my hands are already lifted in praise to you.

Second Chances

I leave so many mistakes in my wake that I have grown to love mornings. I consider each one a second chance to do better and walk more closely in God's plan for me. Learning from our mistakes leads us to wiser choices later. But first we must pay attention to our mistakes. I know that it can seem best to bury them or leave them for others to stumble across. But if we claim them and consider them teachers, we can grow.

God is in the business of transformation. Acknowledge those mistakes and then release them to his custody this evening. And in the morning…use your second chance wisely.

God, you must be tired of seeing these mistakes in my life. Forgive me for the sins that weigh me down. I give the errors, harsh words, white lies, bad decisions, and angry thoughts to you. I did them all. Please transform my mistakes today into stronger character and wisdom tomorrow.

A Life Half Fulfilled

I had a friend who went through a long portion of life without really seeing it. She was heartbroken, but the source of that pain was too difficult to look at closely. Even when we know things are not right, we are not necessarily able to discern what is wrong or what went wrong…all we know is the intimate relationship we develop with pain.

When you examine your life, what do you see? Is it empty? Is it whole and healed? Or have you looked lately? Spend time in prayer. Ask God to reveal what needs to be turned over to him to be repaired and restored.

*I don't want to stop growing or feeling. God,
I need the security of your hope so that I can
safely examine my life. I don't want to be numb
as I carve out a path through the day. I want
passion and purpose. God, fill me up.*

Empowerment

When we decide to live in the light of God, we receive our spiritual superpowers. Okay, that's probably not theologically sound…but our lives are improved, elevated beyond our prebelief existence. We have the power of the Holy Spirit at work in us and through us.

If you are living the same way with the same mind-set, choices, and power features, then you haven't yet started to live the transformed life. Are you afraid you won't recognize yourself if you give everything over to God? Is the "known" of the old, limited existence too comfortable to leave behind? The toughest life choice for some people is their initial acceptance of God—for others it is the decision to live a God-empowered life.

Lord, I want to walk in your light. I see how my way has not allowed for the changes that should take place in my journey. Help me let go of the fears so that I can experience transformation.

Going Home

Our geographic birthplace shapes who we are and notes where we've been. I spent my first eight years in a small Midwestern town that influenced my love for large climbing trees, broad front porches, and summer evenings at twilight.

Our spiritual birthplace shapes who we are and where we are going. You are born in God's heart and in his image and for his purpose. God's breath is your own. His miracles are found in the intricacies of your body and soul. The Creator knows that I love porches and trees and a night sky, just as he knows all about your deepest loves and longings. No matter how far this life journey takes you…you are always home and always heading home. This is the wonder of faith.

You are my birthplace, my journey, my map, my compass, my past, my present, my future, my purpose, my heart, my salvation, my strength, my hope, my security, my joy, and my home. Thank you, Lord.

My Prayer Needs

_____

_____

_____

_____

_____

_____

_____

_____

_____

_____

_____

_____

_____

_____

_____

_____

_____

_____

_____

_____

My Prayer Needs

_____

_____

_____

_____

_____

_____

_____

_____

_____

_____

_____

_____

_____

_____

_____

_____

_____

_____

_____

_____

_____

My Prayer Needs

_____

_____

_____

_____

_____

_____

_____

_____

_____

_____

_____

_____

_____

_____

_____

_____

_____

_____

_____

_____

_____

My Prayer Needs

About the Author

Hope Lyda has worked in the publishing industry for more than 14 years and is the author of several novels and numerous nonfiction titles, including *Tea Light Moments for Women* and the popular One-Minute Prayers series (nearly 745,000 copies sold). When not writing her own books, Hope works as an editor helping others with their writing endeavors.

For more information about Hope and her writing, visit her website: *www.hopelyda.com.*

Hope can be reached in care of

Harvest House Publishers
990 Owen Loop North
Eugene, OR 97402

Or by email at HopeLyda@yahoo.com

Also from Harvest House by Hope Lyda

One-Minute Prayers™

One-Minute Prayers™ from the Bible

One-Minute Prayers™ for Women Gift Edition

One-Minute Prayers™ to Begin and End Your Day

Prayers of Comfort for Those Who Hurt
with art by Annie LaPoint

Tea Light Moments for a Woman's Soul